REDEEMED BY GRACE

Redeemed by Grace

A Catholic Woman's Journey to Planned Parenthood and Back

Ramona Treviño

With Roxane B. Salonen

Foreword by
Lauren Muzyka
Executive Director, Sidewalk Advocates for Life

IGNATIUS PRESS   SAN FRANCISCO

Excerpts from the *Lectionary for Mass for Use in the Dioceses of the United States of America, second typical edition* © 2001, 1998, 1997, 1986, 1970 by the Confraternity of Christian Doctrine, Inc., Washington, DC.

The author changed the names of some of the individuals in her story in order to protect their privacy.

Cover photograph by Lorena A. Jasso

Cover design by Riz Boncan Marsella

© 2015 by Ignatius Press, San Francisco
All rights reserved
ISBN 978-1-58617-914-4
Library of Congress Control Number 2014902186
Printed in the United States of America ∞

To my husband, Eugene, and our children,
Lorena, Savannah, Elijah, and Philip.
You make my life complete and fill every crevice
of my heart with joy.
I love you.

CONTENTS

FOREWORD

God always writes the best stories. I know, because I had the privilege of being a small part of one of his best, namely, this story about my dear friend and former Planned Parenthood manager Ramona Treviño.

On April 23, 2011, my husband, Peter, and I were attending the Easter Vigil Mass at Saint Mark's Church in Plano, Texas, and it was particularly moving because of news about Ramona that I had recently received.

The readings of the Easter Vigil start at the very beginning of time, when God creates night and day, the earth, water and land, the plants and animals, and finally, man and woman. The readings continue, with glimpses of salvation history throughout the Old Testament, and while they are proclaimed, interspersed with the singing of psalms, the entire church is dark and everyone is holding candles, as if to say, "We wait for the light to come."

When the readings turn to the coming of our Lord and Savior, Jesus Christ, as told in the New Testament, the lights are thrown on in a sudden burst of brightness, the choir erupts into strains of "Glory to God in the highest", and one cannot help but feel that everything is different. It's usually then that tears form in my eyes. Yes, everything is different because Christ has entered the world.

The turning of darkness into light especially tugged at my heart that night. Just a couple of months earlier, I had accepted a position with the 40 Days for Life national team as campaign strategist. My job was to advise our campaigns in North America. As a young attorney who loves grassroots pro-life work, I was elated to accept a position that would allow me to use my education, training, and background to serve people who pray in front of their local abortion center—on the front lines, you might say.

In that new capacity, I offered my prayers, support, and advice to the leaders of that forty-day spring campaign, March 9 to April 17, and was constantly in awe of all the amazing things that were happening through God's grace—from babies being saved to facilities closing to workers leaving the abortion business and coming to Christ. But nothing could have prepared me for the beautiful story I was about to watch unfold in the life of one Planned Parenthood abortion-referral worker, Ramona Treviño.

On April 17, the last day of the spring campaign, Gerry Brundage, the director of the 40 Days for Life in Sherman, Texas, invited me to speak at his group's closing celebration. Since Sherman is only about a forty-minute drive from my home in Dallas, and I had developed a friendship with Gerry over the phone during the campaign, I was excited to join his group.

When I arrived at the Planned Parenthood abortion-referral facility in Sherman, I was met by this incredibly kind, warmhearted, and down-to-earth man who shook my hand and welcomed me and my husband with great love. Before the event began, Gerry proceeded to share the many blessings of that campaign. "Oh, by the way," he added, "the manager of this facility and her coworker are thinking about leaving and have already asked us for prayers."

"Wait ... what?" This wasn't something that happened every day. If both women left, it could mean the entire Planned Parenthood facility would shut down. I marveled that Gerry informed me of this development so matter-of-factly, with such faith, as if to say, "Well, we prayed. Of course this would happen." I, however, knew this was something special. I was so excited and filled with hope that after the celebration I immediately texted the good news to our national director, David Bereit, and our campaign director, Shawn Carney.

In the days that followed, Gerry and I talked about how I might help. He forwarded me the résumés of both workers, which I proceeded to share with a small, trusted, pro-life circle in the Dallas area. I'll admit I was a bit nervous, knowing all that former Planned Parenthood Director Abby Johnson had gone through in her exodus from the company, as detailed in her book *Unplanned*. Visions of a lawsuit came to mind. After several days of circulating the two women's résumés, however, nothing seemed to pan out jobwise. I prayed and waited to hear the Lord's guidance for what might be next.

It came that following Saturday night, the night of the Easter Vigil, when the church went from darkness to light. In that moment of illumination, I heard one message very clearly—one I could not ignore: *What could you possibly have to be afraid of? Lauren, I want you to do more.* Recognizing God's voice in my heart, I responded from that same quiet place: *Okay, Lord. I promise to do more. But I ask just one thing. Please protect me.* I felt the Lord's assurance, and assuming the two workers were ready, I made a commitment to do what I could to help them leave Planned Parenthood.

"Gerry, what if I were to call both women to see if I could help? Would you be okay with that?" I asked a few days later. He responded that he had been praying about how to move forward but hadn't gotten an answer, until that moment. Receiving the green light, I immediately turned to my friend and coworker Shawn Carney for insight. After all, he had helped Abby Johnson and would know how to proceed.

Our focus at that point was on the director, Ramona, who seemed more motivated to leave than her coworker. Shawn's advice was simple but vital: "Just let her talk." He encouraged me to listen carefully in order to discern whether she really wanted to make a move.

Within a few days, I was talking with Ramona by phone. Miraculously, by the grace of God, she chose to leave Planned Parenthood about a week and a half later. The Lord had already been moving in Ramona, and it did not take her long to say yes to his promptings. My role was to be a supportive sounding board as the Lord nudged her out of Planned Parenthood and into the new, abundant life awaiting her.

Because of Ramona's choice to leave and the timely decision of Texas to defund Planned Parenthood, that facility closed its doors a little more than three months later. The prayers of the 40 Days for Life in Sherman were answered beyond anything we had even dared to hope.

In the months that followed, I watched Ramona search for, sometimes struggle with, and finally find her true calling in the pro-life movement. By permitting me to be a small part of her inspiring journey, Ramona became a friend and a sister.

Ramona Treviño, you are more than just a former Planned Parenthood manager. You are a wife, a sister, a mother, a friend, and a precious daughter of God. Thank you for being courageous enough to share your journey not only with me but with the rest of the world.

I know you struggled with writing the pages that follow, but you did it because of your great hope that it could touch others who might be wondering if something better awaits them, too. No doubt many insights will come to those who read your story. And in the end, I am most proud of the fact that you did this for the glory of God. I look forward to seeing what the Lord does next in your life.

Dear reader, whatever your faith background, we invite you to join Ramona through the ups and downs of her story—the confusion and questions, the conflict and despair, and, finally, the hope. For those who share Ramona's Catholic faith, I pray you will fall more in love with Christ and the Catholic Church through this story. For those Christians who are not Catholic, I pray that you celebrate the many things you hold in common with your sister in Christ, and that you appreciate her unique walk and the insights that the Lord has given her.

As you prepare to embark on this journey with Ramona, I invite you to find a quiet place, to open your heart, and to see what the Lord has to say to you.

Lauren Muzyka
Executive Director, Sidewalk Advocates for Life
Former 40 Days for Life National Campaign Strategist

A Restless Soul

April 2011

Something wasn't right. I knew it the moment I pulled my hand away from the radio without turning it on. I hardly ever drove home from work without some tunes or a talk show to ease me back into my after-work world. It was just after 7:00 P.M. on Tuesday, but this was my Monday—my first day of the work week as manager of the Planned Parenthood family planning clinic in Sherman, Texas. For the last three years, my routine had been to let the radio accompany me home, but all I wanted now was silence.

"What's wrong with you, Mona?" I said, catching a glimpse of myself in the rearview mirror. "God, help me understand. Why haven't you shown me the way out?"

For the last several months, I had been feeling restless at my job—especially now that God had been revealing so many truths to me. The only time I felt at peace was on the weekends. I would go home and get restored only to face each Tuesday morning with an escalating sense of dread.

When I pulled into my driveway in Trenton, I stopped the car and stayed in my seat. I couldn't go in—not yet. With the keys still in the ignition, I turned on the radio. I wanted to listen again to the Catholic station I had discovered just four months earlier. The programming both attracted and challenged me. The featured discussions seemed to resonate with truth, and that captivated me; yet at the same time, they left me troubled. I wasn't sure if I was ready to confront the possibility that I might have taken some wrong turns.

After all, I was the manager of a contraception and abortion-referral clinic. For three years I had been trying to convince myself that my job didn't have anything to do with abortions—or at least didn't make me directly responsible for them—despite the hundreds of girls I had directed each year to another facility to terminate their pregnancies.

Something that I had heard several times on Catholic radio had been haunting me: "Birth control is the gateway to abortion." The statement bothered me not only because of my own personal actions but also because I had given so much of myself to a place that believed birth control was absolutely necessary for freedom.

"Well, here goes", I said with a sigh, as I turned the dial to 910 AM, Guadalupe Radio Network, landing in the middle of a now-familiar show called *The Good Fight* with host Barbara McGuigan.

Barbara spoke in her usual, soothing voice while addressing a man who had called in—an older gentleman whose loving voice reminded me of my Grandpa Lupe. He was discussing the pro-life work he had been doing, how he had been fighting for years to prompt change, and how important this was to him.

If I had known what was coming, I might have turned off the radio; but since part of me was curious, I waited eagerly for Barbara's response. After all, whenever the topic had to do with abortion, I was all ears, especially since 40 Days for Life had shown up at our clinic during Lent.

Barbara began, "You know, one day we're all going to stand before God, and I believe he's going to say, 'What did you do?'"

I could feel myself tense up.

"First of all, he's going to say, 'Did you know about the pro-life cause? Did you know that over three thousand babies a day were being ripped from their mothers' wombs piece by living piece?'"

I cringed. At that moment, it was as if God was speaking to me through Barbara, and I saw myself now standing before the Lord. It was no longer Barbara but God talking, and not to some random radio caller, but to me.

"And if you say, 'Yes, Lord, I did know', I believe he's going to say, 'What did you do?'"

What did you do, Ramona?

"Oh God," I said breathlessly, "oh, my God." I clutched the steering wheel as if the vehicle were still in motion or as if I might faint in the sudden rush of emotions.

All those months listening to this station, searching for an answer to the question I had been holding deep inside and revealing to no one, not even to my husband, Eugene, arrested me in one clear whisper of truth:

Nothing—that's the answer, Ramona. You've done nothing at all to stop it. Far from it, you've done many, many things to make it possible. Yes, you ... you've been leading babies, along with their mothers, to their deaths, if not of the body, then of the soul. You are culpable.

"No", I said aloud, denying it, yet knowing it was true. "Help me."

Faces of all the young clients I had "helped" during the past three years—pretty girls, sad girls, scared girls—flashed at me. They had walked into our clinic looking for answers, for someone to give them some kind of hope. But I hadn't given them that. Instead, with a smile on my face, I had handed them some brochures about safe sex and a packet of pills before sending them back into the world, vulnerable and destined to repeat the same destructive behavior that had brought them to us in the first place. I hadn't helped them. I had only made things worse for every last one of those precious young women.

My gut began to burn, and in that horrifying moment, it was as if the roof of my car were being unpeeled like the lid on a can of sardines. I sat there feeling helpless, guilty, and completely exposed.

Throughout my life, whenever I felt desperate, I would turn into a little girl again and go to God on my knees, even if only in my mind. The prayers I uttered in such times were not eloquent, nor were they in that moment.

"Oh God," I said aloud, "I'm so sorry." That's all I could muster.

What came from me next can't even be called a cry. It was a gut-wrenching wail, and once it started, it felt as if it would never stop. Realizing I was a mess, I began searching frantically for tissues to dry up the torrent of tears, but they just kept pouring out. I was a wreck. I worried about what Eugene would think if he saw me like this. I didn't want to scare him, and yet, I was scared, truly scared for my soul.

How could I have been so blind? How could I have not seen that I was an accomplice this whole time?

After about fifteen minutes of intense sobbing, I realized if I didn't go into the house soon, Eugene would start looking for me. I glanced once more in the mirror and dabbed at the mascara streaks on my face. Then I slowly got out of the car.

Approaching the house, I paused. Through a window of our home, I could see Eugene sitting on the couch. I took a deep breath, then opened the door and looked around. The kids were asleep already. I was safe at least from their probing glances. Eugene looked up from the television. Worry lines immediately appeared on his face. "Mona, what's wrong?" he said.

I walked over to the couch, dropped my purse, and fell into a spot near him, letting him wrap his arms around me. As he cradled me, I began to let down my guard, to let it all out.

"I'm ... I'm ... I'm going to hell!"

"Why? What happened?" he asked.

I couldn't keep it inside any longer. Everything came out in one jumbled string of words—details of things I had been internalizing for months and keeping mostly to myself. I told him about Catholic radio and 40 Days for Life and reading Abby Johnson's book *Unplanned* and how the people I had always been told were "crazies" really weren't after all.

"It's as if the scales are falling from my eyes", I said. "What I'm doing, Eugene, is wrong. It's just wrong, not only for the people who come into the clinic but for me. My soul is at stake!"

"Oh, it's going to be okay", he said, seemingly at a loss as to how to respond to my strong emotions. "We'll figure it out."

Tightening his hold, he let me cry for as long as I needed and reassured me that everything would be fine, that he would be there for me. Eugene knew I had been restless for a while, and he too had disliked some aspects of my work.

Relieved as I was to be in his embrace now, I couldn't stop the barrage of thoughts charging at me. Was it too late to turn back, or had I compromised my soul forever? What if I were to get into a car accident and die on the way to work tomorrow?

What if second chances weren't possible?

After a while, something interrupted these disturbing thoughts—a calming presence from within, as well as from without. With no other choice, and feeling exhausted now, I began to let that other voice have a turn.

It's not too late.

It wasn't my voice, but it was one I recognized, one that had always been nearby. That's part of the reason I had felt so conflicted. Recently that voice had been trying to reach my ears. I had resisted it at first, but I was finally letting it in.

God had never walked away from me. I was the one who had drifted. I had allowed my sin to blind me from truth. And I had had a hand in abortions—a direct hand. How many girls had I watched walk out of my care and into places that would kill the sweet, innocent lives growing inside them and depending on them for survival? Those girls had come to me with a sliver of hope, searching for a better solution, and I had taken that sliver and smashed it to pieces.

I couldn't wash my hands of any of it; I knew that now. But I also sensed that on the other side of my raw pain, a loving father waited with open arms.

I love you, and I want to bring you to the other side of this; but first, I need you really to look at what you've done and own up to it.

It wasn't too late. I was here, I was still alive, and that meant there was still time. God had spared me so that I could get to this very moment and have a chance to repent and save my soul.

"Thank you for not giving up on me", I whispered.

I went to bed exhausted but filled with newly sparked feelings of hope. But in the morning, I woke up disoriented. Something had changed, but what?

Then I remembered: the driveway, Barbara McGuigan's question, the panic.

I started to feel engulfed again but quickly recalled what had calmed me earlier: *It's not too late. It's not too late.*

I lay there, thinking over various events of the past couple of years, and let my mind wander back to another time I thought the world might come apart. What had brought me back? I was only eight then, but in my darkest moment, God had met me where I was. I learned that night how good it feels when God is near.

How had I drifted so far? I wondered. I needed to retrace my steps to figure it out.

2

Message in the Sky

Fall 1985, Trenton, Texas

It was a cool autumn evening when I met God for the first time.

My parents' angry voices resounded through the neighborhood, rising, falling, and rising again to a crescendo I could no longer bear. I held my hands over my ears, hoping it would all go away, but when I let go, I found that it had only gotten louder.

The argument was taking place a few doors down from our home in another house our family owned and had been remodeling. Did my parents realize that their younger daughter was outside, within earshot? I don't know that it would have changed anything. The bad energy between them had taken hold, and they were locked in, alone in a world of hate.

What the argument was about I don't know. It might have begun with my dad's complaints over my mom's constant nagging. Or maybe the fire had been lit over how he had been drinking away the money set aside for food and clothing. Or maybe Mom had let loose her constant fear that his drinking and driving would land him in jail—again.

To me it was all darkness, blacker than the night before me.

For a while, only muted words emerged. And then I either heard or simply began to feel the word that had always been off limits in our home: *divorce*.

Despite their inability to have a peaceful life together, my parents had always honored the sacrament of marriage. They had made a covenant with each other before God, and they had stuck by it through thick and thin.

That evening, however, I sensed in the volatility of their conversation that my life was in danger. Images of my dad walking out and away forever flashed through my mind. His mother had left his family when he was young, and I knew how it had hurt him. What if he decided to leave us? It seemed more possible than ever before.

As those thoughts entered my mind, I felt like someone in a game of tug-of-war when his opponent lets go of the rope, causing him to hurtle backward to the ground. Warm, wet drops dripped onto my arm—my tears, I realized. I wanted to scream, but I knew that my solitary, small voice couldn't make a dent in that black space.

I looked around, perhaps for some sign of hope, and that's when something shiny caught my eye—a metal ladder propped against our house. I walked over to it and began to climb and climb and climb.

The higher I went, the better I felt. I knew somehow that going up was bringing me to a place of safety. And if I could keep on climbing, maybe, just maybe, I could climb straight into the arms of God himself.

The ladder stopped, and I wriggled my way onto the roof and sat there. I wrapped my arms around my knees, rested my chin on them, and tried to drown out the familiar, angry voices below.

Up there the air felt fresher, lighter, and I looked up into the sky and wondered if God could see me. Clinging to the slim possibility that I might make contact with him, I whispered into the night, "Father, if you're there, if you're real, please, please make this stop." I wanted a sign, something I could see so that I could know for sure that God had heard me.

Off in the distance, the sky lit up like a raging forest fire. It was the kind of lightning that spreads across the sky, announcing itself broadly with quiet booms echoing after it. The suddenness of it both startled and comforted me. And then, it was gone.

Anyone who wasn't there might say, "Well, of course, there was a storm and that's what you saw. It can be easily explained." That could be true. But in my recollection, the night had been cloudless. Even if the physical aspects of the phenomenon have a natural explanation, the timing and awesomeness of what I had witnessed left no room for doubt: God had been listening to my one small voice in the black night. And, as if it had been written in a postscript specifically for me, the lightning had let me know that God had been with me from the start and would never leave.

A peace washed over me like nothing I had ever experienced. It was as if my Grandpa Lupe—or "Papa" as my older sister, Priscella, and I called him—had just pulled a blanket over my sleepy body and stood watch until he knew I was completely asleep. God is real, I thought, smiling for the first time in hours. Feeling satisfied with the answer I had been given, I wiped my face dry, crawled back to the edge of the roof, and carefully began descending the ladder. As certainly as I knew that my Grandpa Lupe loved me, I knew that God had just paid me a visit.

I kept that moment close throughout my childhood, though the strength of it waxed and waned over time. Having received the confirmation from God I had so desperately needed at age eight, I felt I owed him some sort of response for his resounding, comforting message in the sky.

* * * * *

Several years later, when I was about twelve, the 1940s movie *The Song of Bernadette* aired on television, and I was mesmerized. It may have been an old black and white film, but as I watched the true story of the poor peasant girl from Lourdes, France, and her response to a series of apparitions of the Blessed Virgin Mary in the 1850s, I began to fall in love with the idea of living a life for God.

It had been years since God had visited me on the rooftop, but I hadn't forgotten the feeling of being close to the divine. Seeing Jennifer Jones' portrayal of the holy Bernadette Soubirous reawakened my yearning for God. I was in awe of Bernadette's humility and faith.

One part in the movie is especially memorable. To this day, watching it strikes a dagger through my heart. After Bernadette has entered the convent, she comes down with tuberculosis and is suffering greatly, but an older nun assumes she is faking the illness in order to seek attention. Bernadette endures both the illness and the woman's callous treatment with mildness. When the older nun realizes Bernadette wasn't pretending, she has a moment of reckoning before God and begs forgiveness for having acted so self-righteously and judging so wrongly.

I was so moved by Jones' performance that I wanted to be like Bernadette—holy enough to suffer in silence for Christ, so holy that Mary would stop by for a visit. I wanted to be so close to God that I could gaze upon the face of his Mother.

During a commercial break, I looked at Mom and said, "I want to be a nun when I grow up."

"You know, Mona," she said, "I used to have those same dreams when I was around your age." Then she told me about a religious sister who had helped her class prepare for the sacrament of confirmation many years ago. My mother had been in awe of the holiness that showed on the sister's face and the way she treated others with such pure love.

Maybe my mom hadn't become a nun, but who said I couldn't? I decided then and there to be like Bernadette, to give my heart to God in the fullest way possible. That would be my mission. Bernadette stayed etched in my subconscious mind. Though it would be another fifteen years before my confirmation, when it came time to choose a saint's name, Bernadette was an easy and fast choice.

But in the meantime, my childhood dream to live a holy life was dramatically thwarted. At the age of sixteen, I experienced not heavenly signs but very earthly ones—first, a missed period and a nauseous feeling in my middle and, a few days later, a tiny pink plus symbol in the window of a pregnancy test. I stared at the test, feeling light-headed, realizing my life had just changed forever.

3

Protective Embrace

My desire to enter religious life did not go away completely. In fact, even now, I sometimes think that if things were to change and I found myself alone again, I might still be inclined toward this way of total abandonment to God.

But a seed planted in soil without the right nutrients cannot thrive. As a child, I had come to know this from all the times I had followed Papa around in his vegetable garden. In some seasons, conditions didn't lead to a fruitful harvest despite the best intentions. Looking back, I realize my life didn't have the right elements for a religious vocation to grow.

And so it was that I found myself on a divergent course. Rather than moving toward a life devoted to God, I began seeking out another kind of love—one that, in the end, was bound to elude me.

* * * * *

Years before my pregnancy at sixteen, I began to yearn for human love and acceptance.

"Hey, Afro-turf, just how do you get your hair like that?" people at school would tease. "Do you put your finger in a light socket every morning or something?"

The words stung my ears, and I didn't have to look to know they were taunting me. I had heard similar things so many times before. Better not to see the faces of my tormentors.

Growing up in Trenton, I was one of a few Hispanics in a field of Caucasians. Most years, I was the only member of an ethnic minority group in my class, and not only that, but a girl with short, curly hair who stood out in an awkward way.

I first became aware of my differentness on the first day of preschool.
I was looking around the room, searching for crayons or some sign of
the familiar, when two girls approached me.

Were these my new friends? I wondered.

"What's your name?" one of them asked.

"Ramona."

"Oh," the girl said, "um, is that a girl name or a boy name?"

My face felt warm, and my insides tumbled around in confusion.
How could they not know? I wondered. Did I look that much like a
boy?

Unlike Priscella, whose ears had been pierced when she was an infant,
I didn't have pretty gems on my earlobes to make my gender abundantly clear. My short, curly hair also gave me a boyish appearance. And
though I wasn't chunky, my body was naturally thicker than my sister's
lean build, which only added to my feelings of self-consciousness.

Ordinarily, things might have been set right by a supportive maternal
presence, but my mom wasn't one to be emotionally engaged in our
lives. I knew she loved my sister and me. She was always around, never
far away physically. But emotionally she was often distant, too consumed
by my father's alcoholism to be as attentive to us as we needed. I had
quit hoping that she would come to my rescue. The world was a hostile
place, it seemed, and I would have to maneuver through it on my own.

Discovering early on that I was gifted with intelligence, I poured
myself into academics. It seemed the only way I could stand out aside
from being everyone else's joke.

I also began developing a thick outer shell of protection. Though I
was very emotional by nature, I became adept at burying my feelings
deep down. Often, my needs would surface anyway, and I would come
across as demanding attention, which I guess I was.

My bright mind helped but couldn't offer complete solace. I was
often hyper and talkative and easily distracted. Not until adulthood
was I diagnosed with attention-deficit / hyperactivity disorder. In school,
this would often manifest itself as apparent unruliness, which my teachers addressed through constant reprimands.

Still, some of my teachers recognized my gifts and helped to draw
them out. For those teachers I worked extra hard. Especially in verbal
subjects such as grammar and English, I rose to the top of my class, and

in fourth grade, I was placed in a new program for gifted and talented students.

I soared during my later elementary years. Between academics and sports—especially basketball—I had found a way to believe in myself, to prove I was a worthy person. And I desperately needed the confidence booster. School provided an escape from home and my dad's drinking. It's hard for me to admit now, but my sister and I never really wanted him to come to any of our school events. We knew that if he did, he would likely be drunk. Better that he just didn't show up at all.

Despite his weaknesses, I always saw the good man at his core. He had had a difficult life, going from Vietnam War hero to disabled veteran. His artificial hip had made it nearly impossible for him to hold down a long-term job, and he frequently ended up in jail due to his drinking. But he was never violent in any sense of the word. We never felt threatened, physically or verbally.

The alcohol may have numbed my dad's physical and emotional pain, but it only added to the marital strife between him and my mother and made me yearn for what I was missing—a father I could count on at all times.

* * * * *

Although my father wasn't capable of providing all the emotional security I needed, Papa helped to fill the deficit.

My maternal grandparents, who lived next door, provided a haven of sorts. For the majority of our childhood, Priscella and I lived with them, and Papa was everything to me, a living slice of heaven on earth.

My grandmother, who shares her husband's name of Guadalupe, was constantly in the kitchen. Because of this and my sister's love of cooking, the two of them had a good relationship, gathering often to make tortillas, tamales, and other family favorites. But I had taken on the image of a tomboy, which people seemed to want me to be, and was more inclined toward adventure and outdoor activities. And so it was that every spring, Papa would wave me outside to help him with planting his garden. He would walk ahead, making the crevices in the earth, and I would follow behind, dropping in seeds.

"How many do I put in, Papa?" I would ask.

"Oh, just a few—two or three will be good", he would say. And I would do as instructed, comforted by his solid shadow.

Often we didn't even have to exchange words; there was an understanding between us that required only minimal conversation at times. But watching him, being frequently in his presence, I learned many important things, including what it means to work hard and to feel the satisfaction of having done so.

Physically, Papa wasn't foreboding. Like the majority of men in our family, he was on the short side, maybe around five feet, six inches at most, and neither thin nor overweight. To me, he was just right.

What I remember most about him are his hands. They were beautiful and strong—never wrinkly, as one might imagine a grandpa's hands to be. And he had the most gorgeous full head of salt-and-pepper hair. He had a fine moustache, which was also sprinkled with gray, and wore glasses.

When my mom was young, she used to see Clark Gable on television and believe it was her father. Yes, he was a handsome man.

I also loved his embrace. Whenever my sister and I ran up to him, he would give us the biggest, warmest hug imaginable—the kind that makes you feel as if you're in the safest place in the world. His were the arms to which I fled in times of trouble.

During my youngest years, Papa worked about an hour away in Grand Prairie, on the other side of Dallas, helping to build airplane parts, but during most of my growing-up years, he was retired. Yet he was always busy doing something—fixing things around the house or running errands for my grandma, who preferred staying close to home.

Papa provided the missing piece of the puzzle my own father could not offer. It was through him that I came to know there was someplace both strong and soft where I could go in difficult times. He was, in those years, my introduction to the loving arms of God.

But no matter how large a role he played in my life, I knew at some point that he would not be able to follow me into the world beyond Trenton. And so, preparing for that future life, I began to look around, seeking out another kind of protective embrace.

* * * * *

During my eighth-grade year, the gifted-and-talented program at my school was eliminated. With that gone, life became more difficult. I was once again not being challenged in a positive way, and my grades began to suffer. Because I had built my self-worth on academic achievement, any grade lower than an A signaled failure. I had convinced myself that as long as I maintained straight As, everything else wrong in my life could be lived through. But eventually I slipped from top of the class to the number-two spot. When I dipped into third place, I started to panic. I was losing my grip on my world.

It seemed the soil of my life was being tilled; it was turning and changing, being readied for something new, something to help me to believe in myself again. And then, toward the end of my sophomore year, a friend told me about her half-brother Lucio, who was visiting from Mexico. "He's really cute, Ramona. I think you should meet him", she said.

Desperate for a diversion, aching to have someone pay attention to me, I was ready to be swept off my feet by someone tall, dark, and handsome. When he stepped into my life, I made note of his finely chiseled face and blushed at the way he looked at me as if I were the most beautiful thing he had ever laid eyes upon. And it wasn't long at all before I noticed his strong, waiting arms, and wondered how it would feel to be wrapped in them.

Visions of a future life in a convent quickly began to fade.

4

Purple Bruises

Lucio was, by far, the most handsome face in Trenton. That's what I saw then, anyway. Now, I can't help but question my adolescent judgment. As an adult, I've come to understand that real beauty comes from within and radiates outward.

When we started dating, however, the beginning of my sophomore year, I was focused solely on the exterior. It didn't hurt that Lucio was nineteen—by all accounts a man—and from someplace besides Trenton. He had had adventures I could only imagine, and I was ready for new horizons. Perhaps he could bring me to them. And beyond my wildest dreams, aside from his being wonderfully beautiful, he paid attention to me, of all people. Yes, me, tomboy Ramona with the frizzy hair.

His charisma and charm mesmerized me. He even had flowers delivered to me at school one day. "Ramona, you are so lucky", my girlfriends said, making me feel even more special. I had had a few boyfriends before, but nothing like this. No one else had pulled me in so deeply so fast. The chemistry was explosive.

Soon enough, I would learn that explosives can blow up and hurt you.

* * * * *

I was only ten, just about to enter fourth grade, when I began menstruating—the first girl in my class to do so and just on the heels of my big sister, who had gotten her period the year before, at thirteen.

I had watched Priscella closely enough as she had entered womanhood to know what I might expect. When she would cry every month from the pain of cramping, I would taunt, "You're just a big baby."

But then, sooner than I was ready, it was my turn. We were at my grandparents' house when I noticed some bleeding. Since my grandmother was out, I went to the bedside of my aunt Tina, who also stayed with my grandparents then.

"Tina," I whispered, "are you awake?"

She worked nights and was still sleeping, and my voice startled her. When I told her what had happened, she looked concerned, almost panicked.

"Oh, don't worry," I said, "I've already washed my panties and put on a pad."

From her face, I could tell she was surprised, probably because I had seemed so casual about something that should have been a big deal.

Later, when my mom came home and learned the news, her eyes welled up with tears, and she leaned down to give her little girl a hug. I already had other things on my mind by that time.

"Can I go ride my bike?" I asked. "Oh, and this doesn't mean I can't play basketball anymore, does it?"

As soon as she assured me I could continue on as before, I was out the door, ready to resume my childhood.

Though I kept most of this to myself, when school started in the fall, the boys seemed to have noticed the physical changes I had undergone. It wasn't uncommon for them to sneak up behind me in the lunch line and snap my bra. They didn't know what to do with a female classmate who had matured so early. Neither did the principal, who looked at me sideways when I told her I had to go home due to severe cramps.

It wasn't the easiest introduction to womanhood. But a few years later, when the rest of my classmates caught up with me, I felt like an old pro. In many ways, my early physical development contributed to my going places before I was ready. By sixth grade, I had reached my adult height of five feet three, and because my mom didn't fight my wanting to wear makeup early, despite my sister's cries of injustice, I looked older than I was.

In fact, whenever Priscella and I would spend the night with our extended family in Dallas, I would tag along with her and our older cousins and gain admittance into clubs for teens, easily acting the part.

On the one hand, I wanted the attention I had begun receiving, from boys in particular. I learned quickly that I could use my sexuality to draw their eyes my way. And I started wearing short shorts and low-cut shirts to ensure their attention would stay on me.

But on some level, I felt cheap, especially when older guys or men would look at me in a sexual way. Sometimes I would become so uncomfortable I would go home and change clothes and remove my makeup. I was conflicted, not wanting to go without the attention, but not sure I wanted it, either.

* * * * *

Ever since my days of wanting to become a nun, I desired purity and wanted to preserve my virginity, that deeply sacred part of myself, if not forever then at least until marriage. But Lucio's electrifying personality won me over and moved me to reconsider.

One evening, we were at his sister's house, talking about the future. "Mona," he said, "I just don't know if there's anything for me here. I belong in Mexico with my family."

"What?" I said, unable to comprehend what that would mean. "Why? What about us?"

"You know I don't want to leave you, but I just think it's time to go back."

As he said this, he moved in closer, making sure I would know exactly what I would be missing if he were to leave. And in my moment of fear, I succumbed, allowing him to take from me the thing that I most highly regarded about myself—my virginity.

To me, giving up this most precious gift was the supreme sacrifice that said, "Do you see that I love you so much that I'm willing to give this up for you?" It was a skewed train of thought for an unmarried girl, but in my desperation, it seemed the only sure way of keeping him near.

Of course, I can't put all the blame on him, but for me, it wasn't about hormones. He was the first man in my life to pay attention to me, to tell me I was beautiful. After years of feeling insecure, I had a hot guy on my arm and wanted to keep him there as long as possible.

I didn't know my own value, of course. I had missed the memo that before I was born, even before I was conceived, God had marked me as precious. I did not realize that true love would not have demanded what

Lucio wanted from me that night. If only I had been confident enough, strong enough, not to give in to my misdirected emotions.

* * * * *

Lucio and I had been dating only six months when I found myself staring at the pregnancy test, not quite able to believe the result.

It was the summer between my sophomore and junior years of high school, and almost immediately I knew that my intimacy with Lucio had been a huge mistake, that becoming pregnant by this man was not God's will for my life.

Feeding my greatest fear, Lucio went back to Mexico, leaving me on my own to adjust to the reality of a new life growing inside me. I felt lonely and desperate for him to come back. After a few months of begging and pleading, he returned.

As I entered my junior year, my belly protruding, Lucio started showing signs of unwarranted jealously. He didn't want me talking to other guys under any circumstances and did whatever he could to keep me from going to school. I didn't understand it as manipulation at the time.

He did not manipulate with words. Rather, he did it in subtle ways, such as ignoring me when I tried to kiss him good-bye before heading out the door for school. When I got home, he would act as though he were mad at me. He did not explain his anger, leaving me to wonder what I had done wrong. Everything was easier between us when I skipped school and stayed home with him. Soon I began skipping school on a regular basis just to keep the peace.

Given my attention problem, I already had a hard time keeping up with my school assignments. With Lucio's demands and my frequent absences added on top of this, I began to feel hopeless about my classes. Instead of As, I was beginning to pull in Bs—not good enough, not for me. A sinking feeling that I could never catch up academically took over. I began to see myself not as intelligent and capable but as a failure. I couldn't handle what was happening. Feeling suffocated emotionally, I decided to drop out of high school.

And with that, my nightmare began to unfold.

* * * * *

When I was six months pregnant, Lucio and I learned through an ultrasound that we were having a girl. And then I spent the rest of the pregnancy without Lucio. He left for Mexico again, obviously ill prepared to take on the role of a father. By the time I saw him again, Lorena had already come into the world. He had missed the birth of his daughter.

In April 1995, when Lorena was two months old, Lucio and I married in a civil ceremony. Despite our rocky start, it seemed the right thing to do. We had a child now, after all. It was time to grow up.

But in some ways, I realized, life had been much simpler when Lucio was gone. Before, he had found reasons to belittle me, but now, in addition to his jealousy, he began acting out in ways I found disturbing. During an argument, he would bite me or pretend he was going to choke me. This behavior scared me. Even though he would stop short of physical abuse, I was beginning to feel unsafe in his presence.

The red flags were waving, but I waved them away again. I was committed to making our marriage work, for Lorena's sake. The last thing I wanted to admit—to myself or anyone else—was that I might have made a mistake. I pulled out the blinders and hung on tight.

It wasn't long before I couldn't ignore what was happening. I said something ugly to Lucio out of frustration—a comment likely fueled by raging postpartum hormones—and he completely lost it, turning to grab the first thing he could find. It turned out to be a heavy crystal votive cup, which he threw across the room at me full force. It came at me so fast that I didn't have time to move; the sheer force caused it to break apart upon hitting my leg.

The next day, the damage was visible from my knee all the way up my thigh in the form of a huge black-and-purple bruise. Lucio downplayed the whole thing, saying it wasn't a big deal, even convincing me I had deserved it.

"You're right," I said, "it's not a big deal."

By then, I was already feeling too beaten down emotionally to see black and purple for what they were.

* * * * *

I hadn't forgotten about my rooftop experience of God. I knew that all I needed to do was crawl up there again in my mind and watch for the sky to light up. But in my weakness, I had let distractions and competing voices pull me away from him. My earthly needs and insecurities, not God's will, were driving my decisions. Whenever I did turn to God, however, he always provided what I needed; but he waited for me to seek him. Unlike Lucio, God would never force himself upon me.

I began going to my church with Lorena, hoping to hear the pure voice of love that had been drowned out by shrieking and fighting. I would sit in the pew, the same futile prayer always on my lips: "Please, God, change Lucio. Turn him into a good husband and father. I can't continue this way much longer. He has to change."

Sometimes I would feel a strong reassurance that God was alive in my life. I would alternate between feeling that joy and feeling the sheer misery of trying to make things work against the impossible. Eventually, the misery became more prominent.

One afternoon we were out driving, Lucio in the passenger seat and I at the wheel. We had gotten into another argument, and he had backhanded me in the face. I was driving through tears and probably not very straight. A policeman approached from behind, and when he saw the vehicle swerve, he promptly began flashing his lights. He walked up to the side of our vehicle and peered in. "I noticed some erratic driving back there; just checking to see if everyone is okay."

I think he was hoping I would say something to reveal the truth of the situation, but I couldn't. I wouldn't even look into his eyes. I was fearful of the repercussions of speaking out, and I allowed my fear to make me a double hostage.

Later, in learning the patterns of abuse, I realized Lucio had progressed through every stage—possession, manipulation, verbal and emotional abuse, sexual abuse, and eventually full-fledged battery.

* * * * *

When Lorena was four years old my marriage took a turn for the worse. While in Mexico for a wedding, I watched as Lucio flirted with an exgirlfriend. Feeling very jealous and insecure, I quietly fumed the entire time.

By the time we got back to my in-laws' house, it was obvious Lucio was drunk, and I was beyond inflamed. My anger at all the abuse I had been enduring—the hair pulling and scratching and slapping—rose to the surface and sought an outlet. *I'm going to hit him, and I don't care if he hits me back. I'm going to get at least one good one in.* I pulled back my arm and slugged him in the face—a first for me.

I don't remember a whole lot after that, though I assume Lucio punched me back. I do remember the sounds of his sister, awakened and screaming, and being helped into the shower and blood streaming everywhere. I bear the wound to this day—a scar from where he parted my lip and I had to have stitches.

After leaving the hospital, I wanted more than anything to catch a bus home with my daughter. The fact that she saw me in that bloodied state devastated me more than anything else. But his family asked me to stay. To appease everyone and keep the peace, I remained with Lucio for the duration of the visit. But something had changed within me; something had shifted. In my heart, I was done with him.

A couple of evenings later, I made a decision I had been contemplating since returning from the hospital and seeing myself in the mirror. I dialed my parents' number, knowing that what I was about to say would be a full-out lie but feeling that I had no other choice. I couldn't tell them the truth.

"Mom," I said, "I want you to know first that we're all okay, but I was in a little car accident—a little fender bender. I had to get some stitches on my lip."

It was one of many deceits I would feel forced to perpetuate to keep my secret deep within, hidden in the hole where shame, pride, and unhealed wounds fester.

After that last big fight, being intimate with Lucio, with someone who treated me so poorly, was unthinkable. Once, his advances made me feel physically ill; I got up, went into the bathroom, and vomited.

Just prior to my eventual departure, the last phase of the abuse happened: Lucio raped me. He had said a husband can't rape a wife, and I spent years trying to convince myself he was right. But if that were true, why had I been left feeling so violated? Did there need to be violent force for it to be called a rape? Didn't my no mean no? It took me so long to find healing. A damaged soul needs time.

* * * * *

Toward the end of our marriage, I started talking to a priest at the church near our home. I knew something major was missing from my life. Although I had been baptized a Catholic, I hadn't received First Communion; I wasn't able to take part in the Eucharist, nor had I been confirmed in the Church.

"What should I do, Father?" I asked the priest. "What steps do I need to take to become a full participant at Mass?"

He asked if I was married, and I told him I was but not in the Church. He said that I needed to have my union blessed in order to receive the Eucharist, but he spoke bluntly, without tenderness or compassion or any explanation of the Church's teaching.

I left feeling rejected by him and by the Church, and as a result I stayed away from the Church for another year or so. Only later did I realize that my feeling rejected was fueled more by Lucio's refusal to marry me in the Catholic Church than by the meeting with the priest. In spite of my feelings, I continued to pray and to seek God in the recesses of my soul. I needed his help more than ever.

This quiet time with God is when I heard the beginning of an answer. I didn't yet know how I would pull it off, but I knew I needed out of my marriage, for Lorena's sake, and mine, too.

5

God Whispers

"Mona, are you in there?"

My mother's voice was muffled on the other side of the bathroom door in my parents' house, where I had gone to hide. I froze there on the closed toilet seat, holding my face in my hands as if that could hold everything in, keep it all sealed up.

All day long, my insides had felt like water waiting in a garden hose, ready to charge toward the surface and burst forth at the cue—that squeeze of the handle. I just needed someplace safe to let my emotions go where they might, but not so far away that Lorena, now seven, couldn't find me if she needed to.

I had been doing my usual pretending all day, acting as if everything were okay. It had gotten to be quite a game: put on a smile, appear as if you live as charmed a life as, say, Clair Huxtable of *The Cosby Show*, and whatever you do, don't let the inside show on the outside.

The abuse had been hard enough, but there was more to it than that. Lucio had never held down a steady job and worked only when he felt like it, when something compelling enough had motivated him to get off the couch. I had been our family's sole provider during our entire marriage.

And now the weight was bearing down. Each day was like a drama unfolding on a stage, with the curtain going up in the morning and me doing my act for the audience until the final curtain, when I would collapse into bed. I was tired, and the audience seemed restless. The ruse was losing its effectiveness; they were onto me.

Well, at least my mother seemed to be. I let her in, trying to avoid looking directly at her through my tear-soaked eyes. I closed the door behind her, leaned back against the bathroom counter, and dabbed my eyes with a tissue, my shoulders slumped over in defeat.

"What's going on, Mona?" she asked.

"Oh, Mom, I dunno, I'm just ... so unhappy in this marriage. I have been for a very long time. I just don't know what to do anymore."

With the words out, the sobs returned, threatening a torrential downpour. Feeling too weak to stand, I sat down again on the toilet lid, cradling my head in my hands.

"Oh, honey," she said, touching my shoulder gently, "I'm so sorry. I really do understand. I mean, look at your dad and me and everything we've been through. It isn't easy. But that's just how marriage is sometimes, you know?"

That's just how marriage is sometimes. . . . That's just how . . .

Her words echoed through the tiny bathroom as a thin ray from the final light of day streamed through the one small window.

No, no, you don't understand. Dad has never hurt you, not as I've been hurt, not physically. It's different.

I couldn't say the words out loud. It was hard enough for me to admit to myself what my life had become. The shame that had become part of my life—the embarrassment from having allowed things to disintegrate to this degree—had insisted that the abuse be kept secret. And maybe a part of me wanted to protect my parents from knowing how things really were.

I looked up at my mother, searched her face, and suddenly became alert, as if a part of me had just been awakened. Breaking through that awkward moment of silence, I said, "Mom, thank you. I think you've just helped answer a question I've been asking myself for a long time now."

She looked at me, a question forming on her face.

"As much as I love you and Daddy, I don't want Lorena to grow up the way I did, seeing her parents constantly at each other's throats. That's not the way it's supposed to be. I'm sure about that now."

Noticing her pained expression, I felt a pang of guilt, realizing that my honest utterances might have hurt her. But I couldn't help what was happening. It was as if the links from the chains that had kept me from flying, from truly being myself, began snapping open and disintegrating, one by one.

Maybe my mom hadn't been equipped to counsel my sister and me through some of the difficulties we faced while growing up; but in her own pain, she had given me the chance to see what life can be like if you do not rise up and expect more for yourself: miserable.

Now that my vision had been cleared, it was just a matter of figuring out God's will in all this. He promised he would be there, after all; it was my job to listen intently until his voice was abundantly clear.

* * * * *

About a month later, I finally began to hear the quiet voice leading me into my future.

I can't remember where Lucio was, but that wasn't unusual. He often came and went with the wind. Knowing Lorena was safe with her grandma, I retreated into the quiet of our house, relishing the alone time that would allow my soul to go where it needed to go.

Although clarity had come to me in the bathroom with my mother, my feelings of despair had not completely let up. I had grown accustomed to walking around draped in a cloak of depression, and it had become apparent that this was closely linked to my marriage. I knew that if things were to change for the better, something drastic would have to happen.

I didn't know the answer, but I knew who did. In the sanctuary of my now quiet bedroom, I got down on my knees. I began to let it out, just a little at first, and found myself crying uncontrollably. When at last I was totally empty of tears, I lifted my arms and symbolically gave it all to Christ.

I gave him all of my heartache, my struggles with depression, my fears, and even my hopes. I told God that I was very unhappy, that after being married to Lucio for almost seven years, I now realized things were not going to change on their own. Despite my earnest attempts to pray him into change, even God could not change Lucio's heart without his cooperation. Like a little girl on her daddy's lap, I told God I understood now that what was happening to Lorena and me wasn't his will and that he wanted much more for us.

Feeling an overwhelming calm, I was drawn toward the Bible on a nearby desk. I opened it up to a random page and began reading. The passage happened to be 1 John 4:7–21, telling of how, because God loved us so much—enough that he would send his only Son into the world—we ought to love one another.

It had never occurred to me before that loving ourselves should be part of that love for one another; that we cannot love well if we don't start with ourselves. But now, it hit me. Not loving ourselves first would create an incomplete picture of love, rendering impossible our reception of the gifts God wants to bestow on us through his pure love.

As I reflected on this, words began to resound from deep within.

All your life, dear child, you have never loved yourself as you ought. You do deserve more, so much more.

For years, I had been sacrificing myself and my happiness for my daughter, thinking that somehow, like Saint Bernadette, I would be close to God by suffering in silence. I hadn't understood rightly that in order to love God truly and to receive his graces, I needed to begin by properly loving myself.

The voice continued.

I made you, I created you. And you are a reflection of me.

How refreshing it was to hear this, like cool water being sprinkled over my face, washing away the dried-up tears.

"Okay, okay, God, I hear you now," I said out loud, like a resigned teenager talking to her parent, "but how can I get out of this situation without sinning against you? What is the answer to that?"

I didn't know, but God did.

"Dear Father," I said, "if Lucio is not the person you wanted for me, then please show me. If there is any reason I should get out of this marriage, please open my eyes. I don't want to be blind anymore. Please help me. I want Lorena to be happy."

And then, practicing a new skill for the first time, I added, "And, um, Father, I wouldn't mind being happy, too."

All my married life, I had begged God to change Lucio. For the first time ever, I was ready to have God show me what he wanted for me.

Soon, I thought, the answer will come.

* * * * *

A month after I said that prayer, just a day after my seventh wedding anniversary, one of my coworkers knocked on my office door at the county health department, where I did clerical work and other odd jobs as needed. She told me someone at the front desk was asking to talk with me. Since I wasn't expecting anyone, I sensed it might be bad news of some kind.

I recognized his face right away. He was a longtime friend of Lucio. But I had no idea what had brought him here. We walked outside so that we could talk in private.

"There's no easy way to tell you this, Ramona," he began, "but Lucio is having an affair with my wife."

Before reacting, I studied his face. There were so many lies, so many things I wasn't sure I could believe when it came to Lucio's life, but here I sensed sincerity.

"How do you know?" I said. I couldn't respond without knowing more.

"Look," he replied, "I don't mean to upset you, but I didn't want you to be in the dark either."

He went on to explain how he had come across different clues and then finally discovered a videotape that had given him all the proof he needed. While he talked, I could feel the blood rushing from my head as I tried to process what he was saying.

Ironically, perhaps, my first feeling was not anger at Lucio. Instead, it was wounded pride; I felt like the world's biggest fool. Yes, I had often wondered about his fidelity. I had collected little pieces of evidence too. But my suspicion was mostly just worry with no solid facts. Now that the evidence was being laid out, I couldn't help but wonder who else knew, why I had been the last to find out, how I could have been so gullible.

Not knowing what else to say, I thanked him for letting me know.

"Sorry about this", he said.

"Yeah, me too."

After he left, I went back inside to an empty room and called Lucio, who was visiting his parents in Monterrey, Mexico, and asked if it was true. He denied it, but I could tell from his voice that he was trying to cover up something.

After I hung up, I fell to the floor. Tears gushed out at the realization that the beginning of the end had just been prompted. After all, to me, this was the deal breaker, even worse in my mind than the abuse. And maybe that wasn't the right way to think of it. The abuse should have been enough. But that's how much I valued an intimate relationship with someone. I held it in such high regard that to be violated that way seemed impossible to overcome.

I heard a light knock on the door. It was Carmen, my friend and coworker, checking on me. I shared everything with her and began planning how I would respond.

"If I can get a round-trip ticket to Monterrey tonight," I asked, "would either you or Stephanie be able to drive me to the airport?"

"Sure, Ramona," she said, "you don't even have to ask. We're both here for you in whatever way you need."

I booked the flight for that evening, Friday, and called my parents.

"Mom, can you and Daddy take care of Lorena this weekend?"

She too agreed immediately to help, but with concern in her voice she asked, "Mona, what's going on? Are you okay?"

"No, not really," I said, "but I will be; I promise. I'm asking you to trust me. I'm going to be okay, so please don't worry. I'll be back on Sunday night."

Just a few hours later, I was in the backseat of Stephanie's double-cab truck heading to the airport, bawling my eyes out. All I had was a light rain jacket Carmen had lent me.

After a while—and seemingly out of the blue—I started laughing hysterically. Stephanie looked at me in the rearview mirror and then at Carmen in the passenger seat.

"What's going on back there, girl?" Stephanie asked.

I'm sure they thought I had completely lost it. But I couldn't stop laughing and was struggling to speak.

Finally Stephanie asked, "Seriously now, are you okay?"

"Oh, I am. In fact, I'm great!" I said.

Again they looked at me, then at each other, confused.

"It's all good, really", I said. "It's just that, sitting back here feeling sorry for myself, I've had a huge realization. A month ago, I asked God for a sign to show me whether I should get out of this marriage. It took me a while to figure it out, but it finally hit me. God has given the sign!"

Thank you for making it so obvious. Please stay near. I need your strength now more than ever.

I spent the weekend in Monterrey, confronting Lucio in person. He tried to make light of everything, owning up at least to having kissed another woman. But I knew he was trying to protect himself. And in my heart, I also knew that I had flown to Monterrey for one primary reason: to say good-bye, to bring closure to our marriage.

I told Lucio that I was going to file for a divorce. To make things easier on both of us, I said I was doing this so that someday we could start over again. I didn't have any intention of starting over again, however. I lied in order to leave him with a false hope, as he had done to me when I was pregnant with our daughter. I wanted to hurt him for all the hurt he had inflicted on me and for all the times I had felt so utterly powerless. It was my turn to be in control.

Flying back home, I was almost certain he believed that I would forgive him and wouldn't have the courage to go through with the divorce, that good old Ramona would take it again as she had before. But this time would be different. As soon as I could, I called my boss and asked for a day off so that I could meet with a divorce lawyer.

On Monday morning, I withdrew money from a private account I had opened in case I would ever need it. Meeting the lawyer, I laid the cash on the table before her and said, "I'd like to file for divorce, and I don't want child support; just sole custody of my daughter."

"Are you sure?" she asked.

"Yes, completely. She's all that matters to me now."

I would no longer be bound to a life of oppression, and neither would Lorena. We would find our way, together. It would be hard, but I knew it would be possible.

Five months later, in September 2002, our civil marriage was legally terminated. And with that, I was on the way to understanding that when we lay our lives at God's feet and earnestly solicit his will with an open heart, he shows us the way we're to go—his way.

Over time, my vengeful feelings toward Lucio would soften, and I would come to realize that only in letting go of my anger could I ever be truly free. But it would be a process, one in which I would first have to learn I had some of my own weaknesses to overcome.

Indeed, some of the hardest lessons of my life were still ahead of me.

6

Finding Myself, Finding Love

The night the divorce became official, I lay in bed with my arms wrapped around Lorena—or "Lo-lo", as we had taken to calling her—stroking her hair as she slept. All I could think of was how I had made a mess of our lives, especially hers. Had I scarred her forever with my decision to divorce?

From the time she was a baby, Lorena exuded joy. As a toddler, she was a little clown, and in public she would attract the attention of people who would tell me how funny and cute she was. Someone was always gushing over her.

Now, at age seven, she would grab anything resembling a microphone and pretend to sing. She would stand in front of the television and mimic the actors and the singers as if on stage. And she was sharp, absorbing the world around her with obvious pleasure and great interest. She radiated a beautiful presence, for which I was grateful every day.

Would this difficult decision hurt or help her? The implications weighed heavily on my heart.

O God, help me know it's going to be okay and that I haven't ruined Lorena's life.

I closed my eyes, took a deep breath, and reached for the red leather journal I had been keeping since deciding to divorce in order to sort through my emotions. I began writing:

> I never thought I would sit back and watch my baby girl grow up without a father. I pray, God, that my love will be enough for her. I pray that someone will come into her life to show her what a real man is. I pray that someone will come into our lives and will love both of us and take care of us. I pray for happiness. God, I just want us to be happy.

With that, I closed my journal and fell asleep.

33

* * * * *

For the next five months, I felt like a bird with a clipped wing that recently had healed and was finally ready for flight. And yet, something was still wrong with the bird. The scars remained from the injury that had brought her to a place of brokenness.

Burned from all of the messages I had been fed for so long, I still couldn't shake the false ideas about myself that I had come to believe. Rather than grasping that I am a daughter of the Lord, I felt like damaged goods. I had been trained to see myself as an object, and so, not knowing anything different, I presented this skewed version of myself to others.

I began paying a lot of attention to my looks, working hard to shed any weight that made me appear less than perfect, buying revealing clothes, and even carrying myself in a way that invited the wrong people into my life.

Worse yet, instead of pouring life and love into Lorena, I began searching for happiness outside, mainly in the mesmerizing atmosphere of clubs and bars. I even engaged in a one-night stand with a younger man.

A small part of me remained intact enough to know I was dishonoring God by not keeping up my end of the bargain. I had promised him that if he could help me find a better life, I would stick by him and protect Lorena. Instead, I was becoming lost in what felt good.

I realize now that having been a victim of sexual abuse was driving much of this behavior. For so long, I hadn't been in control of anything, including my sexuality. I wanted to regain the power that had been taken from me all those years ago when I gave up my virginity and became a pregnant teen.

One night during this time, I came home from a party at 1:00 A.M. Priscella, who had been watching Lorena, wasn't impressed. She confronted me, almost instigating an intervention-type moment.

"Mona, look at you! What are you doing?" she said sharply and grabbed me as I attempted to walk past her. Pulling away, trying to keep myself steady, I rejected her efforts. "It's my business. Stay out of my personal life!"

But even in my intoxicated state, I knew this was not what I wanted for myself or my daughter.

The next day, in a more sober state, I reflected on the choices I had been making. Yes, I had begun to like myself again, but not in the right way. And then it hit me that I was not only conducting myself in a way that was disappointing God, but also hurting Lorena, this precious child for whom I had been sacrificing all these years.

She had played such a prominent role in my life, even to the point of literally keeping me alive. During my years with Lucio, I had attempted suicide more than once. In the end, what had kept me from going through with it was trying to imagine Lorena's future without a mother in it.

The thought of failing her shook me, and I became determined then and there to recommit myself to being a single mother and devoting myself again to my daughter, who needed me now more than ever.

When my cousin Angela invited me to her best friend's wedding, I was reluctant to go. The last couple of months had taken a toll. I really didn't feel like being social. But I also knew I couldn't hide away forever. Angela had promised me that it would be a family affair and that Lorena was invited as well and could hang out with her cousins. That sealed the deal.

That night, Lucio called to arrange a visit with Lorena, and I ended up mentioning the wedding invitation.

"What's the matter? You don't want to go?" he asked, noting the lack of enthusiasm in my voice. "You should go. I mean, you never know, you might find your destiny there."

* * * * *

The wedding ended up being more enjoyable than I had imagined. I had forgotten how much I loved to dance and how good it felt to be around people I knew were supportive and loving.

Scattered within the group of adults were kids scampering about, dancing to the beat, and adding to the lively atmosphere. At one point, a hip-hop song that was very popular at the time began to play, and a big group of us women pulled each other out onto the dance floor.

While there, I spotted a handsome guy dancing by another group but off to the side a little. On a high from the fun energy, I was feeling courageous, so I maneuvered my way over to him, and we started dancing together. A salsa song followed, and we decided to keep dancing through that and a few others.

When the man smiled, I noticed he was wearing braces, which I thought was incredibly charming. And even though I had purposefully not been looking for a date, I found myself wishing he would at least ask me my name. Maybe he can't speak English, I thought.

Eventually I would learn that the mystery man hadn't talked to me because he had assumed I was a snobby, stuck-up woman. Not only that, but he was still reeling, as I was, from a difficult relationship, one that had not included marriage but had given him a daughter, Savannah, who was close in age to Lorena. Like me, he was wounded and deeply guarded.

But it didn't feel right to leave without thanking him for the dances at least, so before Lorena and I left, I looked around for him to say good-bye.

"Hey, um, I didn't catch your name," I said when I found him, "but I wanted you to know ... that was really fun. Thank you."

"No problem," he said with a smile, "and it's Eugene."

Ah, so he does speak English, I thought. My face felt warm as I turned with a shy smile, grabbed Lorena's hand, and headed out the door. As we got into the car, I thought, "Well, that's the last I'll see of him."

* * * * *

A few weeks later, Angela insisted on throwing me a twenty-fifth birthday party—a costume party since it was so close to Halloween—at her home in Dallas. She knew I had been through a lot and wanted to do what she could to cheer me up.

What I didn't know then, and what Eugene didn't know either, was that Cupid was at work. Apparently Angela and her friend Amy had conspired to have the two of us meet, since we were both single, had daughters close to the same age, and seemed to them like a good pair.

"Mona, remember that guy you were dancing with at Amy's wedding, Eugene?" Angela asked a few days before the party.

"Yeah?"

"Well, put it this way. He didn't exactly have an awful time dancing with you. So, um, I sort of invited him to your birthday celebration. I hope that's okay."

"What? You're kidding", I said, a bit confused but a little excited too.

"Hey, don't worry about it. No pressure. If nothing else, you could make a new friend. No harm in that, right?"

I later learned Eugene had been told that I was the one who wanted to meet him. Neither of us realized we were being set up.

I arrived at the party dressed as a belly dancer with my little butterfly, Lorena, at my side. And sure enough, Eugene had shown up too, wearing a nice outfit, no costume, and looking quite handsome. But as the night progressed, I noted that, for a guy who had reportedly enjoyed my company so much just a few weeks ago, he sure seemed aloof.

"I'll bet he's a jerk after all", I mumbled to myself.

I tried to shut him out of my mind. After all, I wasn't looking for a guy. This must be the way things were supposed to be. But then, just as I was set to move on, I caught his eye from across the room. I could have sworn at that moment someone was whispering in my ear, "Go to him."

Go to . . . what?

Go to him.

The feet that walked over to the nice-looking man in the corner, it seemed, weren't mine. Even the words that came out of my mouth seemed to be from someone else. But once we started talking, we couldn't stop. We bantered for hours, paying little attention to anyone else. When he asked if he could call me, I jotted down my number on the closest scrap of paper I could find and said with a smile, "And try not to lose it."

That smile stayed with me. I wasn't making wedding plans, but the evening had given me hope that a good relationship with a man was possible, that I needn't give up altogether on the possibility of love.

It wasn't long before Eugene and I started dating, though both of us were cautious and proceeded slowly, for our daughters' sakes as much as anything else. When Lucio heard about this, he was furious. "Don't you realize he only wants you for one thing?" he said. "No man is going to want a woman who already has a child."

But Lucio's power over me had lost its effectiveness. Eugene was different. I could feel it. Even in the short time I had known him, he had honored me in a way Lucio never had. This time, I was going to ignore the voice that came at me like poison and pay attention to a different voice, the one within.

Perhaps realizing that all hope of our getting back together was now lost, Lucio cut himself off from Lorena and quit making any significant attempts to be a part of her life. Despite some sadness over this, I sensed deep inside, for the first time, that everything was going to be okay.

* * * * *

Two years later, on September 11, 2004, Eugene proposed. It was a huge surprise, and I said yes; and we began planning immediately. I quickly learned that Eugene had dreamed of being married in the Catholic Church and that for him, marriage was a once-and-forever commitment.

The following year, we began classes to enter the Church formally. We discovered through discussions there that by engaging in premarital relations, we had been committing a grave sin. Wanting to honor our faith and its teachings, we made a commitment to remain chaste until our wedding day.

It was a true blessing to me that Eugene was willing to overlook his more immediate desires in order to honor God. This was something I had never witnessed before in a man. And I wanted to honor God in this way as well. We couldn't undo what was already done, but through God, all things are made new. It was a fresh start.

During this time, I came to understand more fully the nature of Christian marriage, and I learned that I had not been in a sacramental union with Lucio. Because I had not been married in a Catholic ceremony, my marriage to Lucio was not looked upon by the Church as valid, leaving me free to marry Eugene without going through the annulment process.

An even bigger blessing was going to reconciliation for the first time and feeling God rub away the grime of our hearts and souls, allowing us to walk into our new lives with clean consciences.

I was so ready to settle down. My life with Lucio had never been settled, and it was time for something stable. In my heart of hearts, I also desired to have more children—with a man who could offer true fatherhood.

Eugene was the answer to my prayers, and our wedding was everything we could have hoped for. On June 3, 2006, we married in the Cathedral Shrine of the Virgin of Guadalupe in downtown Dallas, a church in which I had dreamed of getting married since I was thirteen, after attending a cousin's wedding there.

How good our God is, I thought. He made my heart's desire for a wedding at the cathedral come true. But even better, he had answered our prayers for our children: providing Lorena with an amazing step-father and allowing me to become a stepmother to Savannah. In the sacrament of marriage our families were not only united but enlarged; we each gained a new daughter that day—icing on the wedding cake.

Finally, things were happening in the right order and the right way. "Thank you, God", I whispered while throwing my bouquet into the crowd.

7

Planned Parenthood

My first job after leaving high school was as a teacher's aide, a job I held for three years until Lorena was almost three. From there I moved on to another government job with the county's Women, Infants, and Children (WIC) program.

Despite varying levels of satisfaction in these positions, something always seemed to be missing. More than anything else, I yearned to help others in a more direct way, especially those in situations similar to what I had experienced as a young mother.

My work for the county spanned seven years and involved several roles, the longest of which was an eligibility clerk for women seeking supplemental food for their young children.

Though the security of a government job was comforting, every so often something would gnaw at me.

You don't have enough power here to make a real difference, Ramona. You aren't doing enough to help people. You could do so much more.

My supervisor Denise, whom I adored, entered an arduous battle with cancer, eventually succumbing to it. With her gone, I discovered quickly I had less tolerance for aspects of the job that had frustrated me. Apparently part of my reasoning for hanging on so long had hinged on Denise's presence.

Soon enough, it also became obvious that my moving up the ladder within the organization wasn't on the minds of those who could make that happen. Finding myself at a dismal dead end, I up and quit. Leaving the job did not give me peace, however, and left me with a feeling of having burned some bridges—a feeling I soon would go overboard to correct.

Just a couple of weeks later, I learned I was pregnant with Elijah. And shortly after that, Eugene lost his job. We had been staying with my parents, saving up to buy a house, but now with no income of our own, we applied for government assistance.

God came through for us in many ways at that time. For one, Eugene's jobless state lasted only six months. But our feelings of vulnerability left an indelible imprint. I knew that I would have to return to the work-force soon.

I did accept a part-time job during my pregnancy, taking care of seniors in their homes, but as my belly grew, straining my back, the work became impossible; I had to leave that job too.

Elijah came into the world two months premature, in February 2007, and I stayed home to care for him during his first year, relishing every moment with my baby boy. But with each passing month, the realiza-tion of our limited finances weighed heavily on me.

Then, in March 2008, I received a call out of the blue from my friend and former coworker Nancy, who recently had left the county agency for another job.

"Hey, girl, how's it going?" the familiar voice said. How good I felt to hear it once again. There wasn't a lot I had missed about my old job, but I had missed Nancy.

She sounded so positive and excited while telling me about an open-ing within her new company, Planned Parenthood. Not only was it part time—perfect for me—but it apparently came with advancement opportunities.

"Ramona, they are always looking for people who want to move up to be managers and directors", Nancy said. "I really think you'll love it. And you're going to be helping mainly low-income women, just like you've always wanted."

My interest was piqued as Nancy continued to share information about the position—how I would learn to do blood draws and to take blood pressures: new skills I could add to my résumé. It sounded like valuable work that would be both challenging and rewarding and cer-tainly more important than anything I had done before.

At the time, I was largely ignorant about Planned Parenthood. As a young mother, I had been mainly absorbed in work and family. Public discussions concerning abortion and the connection between Planned Parenthood and the abortion industry were simply not on my radar. Like many, I believed that the organization's primary purpose was to help women.

After Nancy had finished rattling off all the benefits of the company, she mentioned that the clinic for which she worked, as well as the one near me that had an opening, had no connection whatsoever to abortions. I thought it a bit odd that she mentioned that, since the possibility hadn't even crossed my mind. Of course, I would never want anything to do with abortions. Like Nancy, I was Catholic. It was hard for me to fathom that the abortion industry even existed, not to mention that people would choose abortion. Later, I would understand better why this had been such an important point to Nancy. But at the time, I was oblivious.

"Ramona, I've really missed you," Nancy said, "and just think, if this works out, we'll get to hang out again from time to time. Remember how much fun we used to have?"

The thought of working with her in any capacity made me even more open to the possibility. "Well, I guess it wouldn't hurt to interview, right?" I said.

The one drawback was that there would be a bit of a commute, but I chose to overlook that, knowing that in time I could move to another location closer to home. After filling out an application at the Gainesville branch of Planned Parenthood, I took part in a phone interview, which led to an in-person interview a few days later at the company's Dallas branch. I had applied for the position of assistant. I could start there, I figured, and just as Nancy promised, move up by proving myself worthy.

The interview went well. I felt as if I had answered everything as explicitly as possible. The only thing left to do was wait out front with the others to be called back in for a post-interview discussion. As I waited nervously, I let myself dream, just a little, of my new future and of how this change might even help me to be a better mother and wife.

Everything was about to change; I could sense it.

"Ramona," said the human resources coordinator, interrupting my thoughts, "would you like to come back here and discuss your application?"

A rush of excited energy charged through me as I followed her back to the interview room.

"Well," she said, "we've looked at all of your qualifications and appreciate what you shared in the interview. We'd actually like to offer you a position today, but ..."

My heart skipped a beat. But *what*? I wondered.

"But rather than having you doing something for which you're clearly overqualified, we're wondering if you'd be interested in managing our Sherman location? It's obvious to us you have what it takes, and we're looking to expand our clinic, bring it to the next level. Ramona, we feel that you'd be the perfect candidate for this. What do you think? Would you be up for it?"

I tried to contain my excitement. In my mind, I was stepping onto a platform, with the spotlight on me, and being given the authority to make decisions that would affect lives in a positive way. It was everything I had ever wanted. Even the pay, though less than what I had been making at WIC, was certainly more than I had been making by staying at home and would be a good starting point. Plus, I would be obligated to work only three days a week—an ideal fit for a busy mother.

"I do have to ask you just a few final questions", my interviewer said.

"Sure." I was ready at that point to tell her anything she wanted to hear. Though I hadn't yet uttered the words of acceptance, I had already made up my mind that I wanted the job.

"How do you feel about Plan B?" she asked.

She must have noticed the confused look on my face.

"In case you don't know what that is," she said, "Plan B is an emergency contraceptive."

After hearing her explanation, I rattled off the best impromptu answer I could muster. Whatever I said, it must have been good enough for her.

"I think this is going to work out nicely, Ramona", she said, extending her hand. "Welcome aboard."

Indeed, the offer had exceeded all my hopes. I floated out of the place, barely able to keep myself grounded for more than a few minutes.

Ramona the manager—now that has a nice ring to it.

On the drive back to Trenton I cranked the tunes, a huge smile on my face.

* * * * *

April 2008 was my first official month at the Sherman Planned Parenthood facility. For the first couple of months, I spent all my time and energy becoming versed in what I would be doing in my new role, and I was eager and ready for the challenge.

I would be responsible for much of the day-to-day running of the clinic, such as taking care of the financial reports and other office work, including manning the front desk when needed. With limited support staff, the job would be very hands-on, and all the employees would have to work together, taking turns checking patients in and out, answering the phone, and making sure that the clinic was stocked with supplies and that the deposits at the end of the day were correct. In addition, I would have to keep track of employees by doing regular reviews of their performance and hiring and firing when necessary.

All of these duties fell in line with what I wanted, and I couldn't have been more thrilled. Being in charge in this way meant that I could treat people the way they deserved to be treated—the way I would have wanted to be treated if our situations were reversed. I was determined to be an excellent manager, just as I had been determined to be a straight-A student. What I would soon learn, however, was that the disappointment of getting a B as opposed to an A was nothing close to the distress I was about to face.

* * * * *

Every closet of every soul includes at least a few skeletons—those actions we would reverse in a second if it were possible. But sometimes those regrets, as painful as they are, hang around to serve as important reminders of where we have been and how far we have come.

One particular skeleton haunts me from time to time, and it should. This one wears a sash marked with the words "Ramona's First Abortion Referral", and it seems intent on not letting me forget where a wrong turn or twist in logic can lead.

From early on in my time with Planned Parenthood, I knew that abortions took place in their larger facilities in Dallas and Fort Worth. But the Planned Parenthood Federation of America umbrella was huge, and its larger facilities—the "surgical health services" branches that performed abortions—seemed like completely separate entities from the smaller clinics that did not perform abortions. I had made that distinction early on because it is what I believed at the time and it allowed me to enter the organization with a clear conscience.

But only after a couple of months on the job, there came a day when I could no longer draw that distinction so easily. It was a Wednesday, a pill-pickup day, when we were without our nurse practitioner and not seeing patients. Instead, we were refilling prescriptions, administering walk-in pregnancy tests, and taking care of administrative obligations.

When the young college student and someone I guessed might be her boyfriend came in for a pregnancy test, our family planning assistant was busy auditing patients' charts. The student explained to me that she had already taken a home test and wanted confirmation from us of its accuracy. I handed her the required forms to fill out and collected the twenty-five-dollar fee.

"I'll take her back", I said, nodding to the assistant. "You just keep doing what you're doing."

To me, being "the boss" didn't exempt me from rolling up my sleeves to help. We were a team, and it was important to convey that message right away. So when the client had finished filling out her paperwork, I was happy to bring her back to begin the test. It sort of felt good to be doing some hands-on work with a client. After all, that's why I had taken the job—to help people.

I escorted her down the hallway, showed her the restroom, and handed her a small plastic cup in which to leave her urine sample. When she was finished, I led her to the exam room to wait for the results. She asked if her boyfriend could join her, and I showed him to the room so that they could wait together.

When the test came out positive, I quickly gathered the paperwork that was to be given to patients with positive pregnancy tests, along with a few pamphlets on prenatal care, then retraced all the necessary steps to make sure I wasn't forgetting anything important. Then, with the materials in hand, I went into the exam room, sat down in the chair next to her and smiled.

"Congratulations," I said, "you're pregnant."

She immediately began to cry, which took me by surprise. I sensed the boy fidgeting in the chair behind me, though he wasn't saying anything.

Did I say something wrong? Oh no, did I miss something?

I looked over her paperwork again and spotted something I had overlooked the first go-around. She had checked the word "abortion" as her choice of referral.

Scrambling to find the right words, I immediately apologized for my oversight. I wanted to respect her choice, after all, and honor what I had been trained to do in these situations, which was to give patients the information for abortion-administering sites. That was simply protocol.

Along with the two Planned Parenthood facilities in Dallas and Fort Worth, the list included several others where late-term abortions were performed, but they were privately owned.

Even while trying to stay composed, I could feel my tangled emotions trying to have their way. Somehow I had fooled myself into thinking I would never actually be in this situation, that I would bypass it. But there I was, searching for a way to be a good employee while being faced for the very first time with the raw reality of abortion. I had never even met anyone who wanted an abortion; but now she was staring me in the face, and I couldn't dodge her. Someone I was helping was actually considering killing her baby.

A rush of thoughts came at me in what seemed like a fraction of a second as my mind whirled with what to say and do next.

Get it together, Ramona. You need to find a way around this.

"You know," I began, "abortion is a very difficult decision that shouldn't be made so quickly. Maybe you want to take a little time before you decide?"

"I've already made the decision", she said, still distressed.

Good Lord, I'm not trained for this. I'm not a counselor.

"At the very least," I said, "you should really have a support system in place before you go through with this. Do your parents know?"

"My parents can't know. They'd kill me if they knew."

"Does the father of the baby know?" I asked. Though her boyfriend was right there, I couldn't automatically assume he was the father. "Will he be there for you during and after? You should really discuss this with him."

She looked at the young man in the chair nearby and then back at me. He still hadn't spoken.

"Yes, this is the father," she said, "and we've made this decision together. This just isn't the right time for us."

What else could I say? I couldn't force her to change her mind; that would be totally out of line. So, I handed her the paper listing the abortion clinic names and numbers and wished her well.

Escorting the two down the hallway, I stopped at the entrance door, and as I held it open, I watched them slowly exit out of my sight, tears still streaming down her face, his head hung low.

Now at a safe distance from them, I could let down my guard a bit, and as I did, the rush of emotions came back. As tears began to well up in my own eyes, I quickly slipped into my office, hoping no one had noticed, and shut the door. Leaning against the other side of the door, I began to sob uncontrollably.

"What's wrong with you?" I asked myself. "It's her choice, isn't it? You're not here to judge anyone, right? Who knows if she'll even go through with it? And why are you crying, silly? It's part of your job. It's not you doing the abortion, after all."

I began wiping away my tears, but the thoughts continued. I told myself how stupid I was for falling apart. After all, I hadn't encouraged her to get an abortion. No, on the contrary, I had asked her to think about it, right? The final decision was hers, not mine. And her choice would be between her and God. She, not I, would stand before him and answer to him one day.

With that, I threw my crumpled tissues in the garbage, took a deep breath and headed back to my desk.

Someday this moment would haunt me. But for now, I would tuck it away and pretend it had never happened.

I went on doing my job as I had been trained, and as further abortion referrals came in, it wasn't long before I had nearly forgotten about my little emotional breakdown. Like Pontius Pilate, I was just fine with washing my hands of that first abortion referral and all those that would follow.

Yes, I was always sad when women chose abortion. And in moments when I was experiencing spiritual unrest, I would even say a little prayer for them—an act I now see as hypocritical. But I had a job to do, bills to pay; the ultimate decisions of these women couldn't be my worry. I had to push on.

* * * * *

By this point, my honeymoon phase at Planned Parenthood had ended. Aside from the gut-punch of that first abortion referral, and the ambivalence I experienced with those that followed, other perplexities had cropped up, causing me to question whether I had stumbled onto my dream job after all.

For one, a pattern of management instability had emerged. The supervisor with whom I had originally worked quit a few months after I was hired. In fact, area managers were often shuffled around; I never had the same one for very long. During my three years at Planned Parenthood,

I worked with four different supervisors, all of whom covered several clinics at once, leaving them little time to check in with me.

With this turnover came continual changes, a constant revision of rules, and much confusion among the staff as to what our roles were to encompass. Each manager had a slightly different approach to how things ought to be run. Just as I was making a connection with a supervisor, she would be assigned to a different clinic, and I would need to start all over again. As a result, I found it difficult to stay on top of things.

A bright spot came with the arrival of my second family planning assistant. I immediately took a liking to Linda, who was in her early fifties and as nice as she was attractive. I enjoyed hearing about her adventures as the daughter of a professor and learning about her aunt who was a nun. In her earlier years, through her father's career, Linda had had a chance to travel the world, and I loved listening to the stories she had collected along the way.

Like me, she was an independent woman with a strong personality, which was balanced by a caring nature. She was drawn to medicine because of its capacity for healing and helping and thrived on learning new things. Though I was her supervisor, oftentimes I sensed Linda was the one doing the guiding.

She had also experienced years of being a single mother and was very involved in the life of her two children. These commonalities provided a base for a warm relationship. In the work environment, she was particularly adept at knowing when it was time to get down to business and when the moment called for a lighter mood.

Aside from the presence of Linda, a few other perks made my job tolerable. Wednesdays, for example, were administrative and pill-pickup days. Since the clinic opened only for pregnancy tests and walk-ins, we could focus most of our time on paperwork, finances, and organization.

When I began at the Sherman site, we were in the red financially and seeing only three or four patients a day. By my second year, over twenty patients were coming into the clinic daily, and our financial picture had drastically improved. I couldn't help but feel proud that I had been largely responsible for turning things around.

But the growth had come at a cost: I believed that we were understaffed and overworked.

The first year went by in a blur, with me spending most of my time learning the ropes and figuring out where I could make immediate improvements. During the second year, what I thought were staffing problems came into focus. When I tried to bring these to the attention of the administrative layer above my own, however, my pleas for help seemed to fall on deaf ears, and the burden of overwork fell on me and my staff.

"Hey, Linda, you need your lunch break", I would often say.

"What about you, Ramona? Don't you need to eat?" she would respond.

"Oh, don't worry about it. You're working your tail off. You need it more than I do."

After all, I reasoned, Linda was older than I. It wouldn't be responsible or fair for me to deny her a little midday reprieve. I would take the hit for the team.

When I did have a moment to sneak in a lunch, I would usually scarf down my food in ten minutes. I just couldn't bear to see people waiting in the lobby or to hear the phones ringing off the hook while I enjoyed a leisurely meal in the back.

In time, however, I started wearing down. The pressure I was feeling to push the numbers and to fill the schedule without any increase in help to handle the rising workload began to catch up with me. As a result, I found myself doing something unexpected: I began pushing back.

8

Pill Pusher

Through all the disappointments with my job that second year, one good thing I had hoped for did come to fruition: I was back in contact with Nancy, who became my main source of support. Linda also had a sympathetic ear and was nurturing to me in many ways, but because I was her supervisor, I felt I should be careful about what I divulged to her.

From all outside accounts, things were going well for Nancy. Driven like me, she had proven herself to be a hard worker and had been rewarded by being made manager of the McKinney clinic. As fellow managers within the same company, we would often call one another, comparing notes and commiserating occasionally.

Sometime in the middle of that year, we began challenging one another, engaging in what we considered friendly competition.

"Okay, Nancy, here's the deal", I would begin. "Today I'm going to see if I can get twenty-three patients into my clinic. Bet you can't top that!"

She would counter with her own goal. "We'll see. Just watch me go. I'm going to beat that by two!"

These little games weren't entirely our own idea. Our supervisors had promised that if we could prove that we needed an extra employee, we would get one. Nancy, who felt as burdened as I with the perceived lack of support, took the offer to heart and started busting her bottom to one-up me.

We went back and forth in this manner for several months before I began to grow weary. Both our numbers were increasing, but no new employees had appeared to help us with our daily tasks.

The situation seemed to be taking a toll on Nancy, too, whether or not she wanted to admit it. She had been suffering some health

concerns, and I couldn't help but wonder how much of it was tied to
work pressures.

One day, exasperated by it all, I just threw it out there. "You know,
Nancy, this is downright ridiculous. I mean, do you really believe this
is getting us anywhere?" I asked. "Personally, I just don't think I can do
it anymore. And I don't think we will ever have more staff. It's futile."

"Yeah, you're right, Ramona", she admitted. "It's not worth it."

Still, I couldn't have guessed that not long after that, Nancy would up
and leave Planned Parenthood.

* * * * *

When the McKinney clinic opened, it was brand-spanking new and
quickly attracted attention from the pro-lifers in the area. A prayer circle
started gathering at the facility each week, and Nancy began stepping
outside from time to time to pray with them. We learned later that they
were praying for Nancy, with the hope that she would leave her job.

With a newly opening heart, Nancy began seeking counsel from her
parish priest, sharing concerns about her workplace; and in the course of
those conversations, he encouraged her to leave Planned Parenthood. It
didn't take Nancy long to find another job, and by the end of that year,
she was gone. Since she had been the one to woo me to the organization, I couldn't help but feel unsettled—not to mention sorry for myself.

By the time Nancy left Planned Parenthood, other things about my
job had begun to trouble my conscience. From the beginning, Nancy
had assured me that my work would not be tied to abortion in any way,
and yet another disturbing connection began unfolding before me, situation by situation.

Our clinic was dispensing contraceptives to minors without the con-
sent of their parents. We were treating girls as young as twelve as if they
were responsible adults. If I couldn't even convince Lorena to take her
vitamin every day, what sense did it make to entrust young girls with
taking daily pills to prevent pregnancy? And if they forgot to take them
or took them improperly, which was likely, how could we not expect
them to seek an abortion? The lines that had seemed clear before were
beginning to blur.

Helping me to connect the dots was the fact that my own daughter,
whom I wanted desperately to protect and to guide, was now reaching

the age of many of those I was presumably helping by nudging them toward contraception. It bothered me to think that Lorena could walk into a neighboring clinic and ask for pills so that she could have sex with Lord knows what man or boy who had been successful in convincing her that he truly loved her, just as Lucio had convinced me when I was not much older than she.

One afternoon, a girl of about fifteen came into the clinic with her dad. Despite having had only one sexual encounter, she had contracted herpes. Because of her embarrassment, she waited to tell anyone about the symptoms, and by that point, the disease was so advanced that she could not even sit down.

Hardly anyone left our clinic without hearing about "safe sex" practices and receiving a pack or two of condoms. Yet, despite our attempts at education, the girls kept coming back with scared looks on their faces, seeking help and answers, for they were experiencing the effects of STDs.

In one particularly heartbreaking case, a young woman engaged to be married had contracted an STD by sleeping with some random person one drunken night of partying. Her fiancé didn't know about it, she sadly revealed, obviously ashamed.

Young women or girls were not the only ones being harmed. A young man with same-sex attraction came into the clinic HIV positive and wanted to be tested for other STDs. He was negative for the other diseases, but when he returned six months later, he tested positive for chlamydia. Our nurse practitioner told him it was more likely that the other diseases, if contracted, would kill him before the HIV, because they were becoming resistant to antibiotics. A sick feeling came over me as he walked out the door, not any better armed against disease than when he had come in the first time. Wouldn't he have benefited more from being referred to a counselor who could help him to live a chaste life?

There were so many things coming into view that I could no longer avoid. Yes, it was true that our clinic did not do abortions. But what about our clients who had either discovered or received confirmation of a pregnancy and were sent away, by us, with the phone number for the closest abortion facility? I began tossing and turning at night, wondering why we couldn't help these scared girls—take them by the hand and tell them about other options that would not lead to the deaths of their children.

No matter how much I tried to convince myself that I wasn't partic- ipating in abortion, the evidence against that seemed to be mounting. The abortion referrals were a particularly glaring example; it was becom- ing harder to let that slide off my back. Always a seeker of truth, I had to ask the questions and to go wherever they led me, whether I liked the answers or not.

I argued with myself about the messages we seemed to be sending through our actions, even if not explicitly: "You're destroying your life by using these drugs, but I'm going to keep selling them to you any- way because I'm making money off you"; "You're destroying your life by being promiscuous, not remembering who your partners were and exposing yourself to sexually transmitted diseases, but here's a pill to help you to stay in that cycle."

The mother in me who had come to the clinic to protect girls, and who had a girl of her own to protect, was struggling with reconciling the divergent messages—the one in my heart and the one I was doling out to our clients. Why were we not saying to these young individuals who came to us in desperate situations seeking help, "This isn't good for you; this isn't healthy for you; there's another way"?

At the end of that year, Planned Parenthood organized a Plan B competition. Apparently there had been an overstock of the drug, and they needed to get rid of it before it expired. The way to do that, they decided, was to encourage the clinic directors to sell more of it. To motivate us, they told us that the director of the clinic that sold the most Plan B would earn a prize—a fifty-dollar Visa gift card.

Who would turn down a little extra cash? At first I was gung ho, charged up by the thought of a shopping trip all for me. But then reason kicked in, and I recognized that I was being tempted to sell Plan B to clients who might not need it.

Later I realized that many of the locations funded by the government were winning all of the gift cards. These clinics were able to sell the most pills because their clients were covered by public insurance programs that included Plan B. Because our clinic wasn't funded, we didn't see a lot of Medicaid patients, for example, so I began to feel that the compe- tition was unfair.

But something else was troubling me. Were all the Plan B pills being sold medically necessary? If there were cases in which they were not, what would be the difference between our clinic workers and the pill pushers who infiltrated the seediest parts of town to sell prescription drugs on the street corner?

During the height of the competition, Planned Parenthood was dishing out nearly $2,000 worth of gift cards to employees each month.

Why can't they just give us a raise? I wondered.

9

The Girls of Grayson County

In the spring of 2010, a call came into the clinic from a Grayson County social worker, and I happened to be the only one free to pick it up. In their juvenile detention facility, the county had been seeing a rise in teen girls who had been impregnated by older men, the social worker explained, and she wanted to know if Planned Parenthood offered any kind of sex education program to help them.

One of the first questions I asked was whether the girls had reported the names of their older boyfriends, since some of the cases likely involved statutory rape. The social worker said that the girls wouldn't release the names of the fathers, in order to protect them. Furthermore, many of the girls were in vicious cycles of abuse or being raised by grandparents short on resources. Without any better solutions, the county authorities believed that educating the young women about responsible sex would at least slow down the rise in the pregnancy rate.

I was moved by the thought of these girls and the desperation they must have been feeling. During the course of our conversation, I became determined not to hang up without offering something, even though I felt a bit out of my league.

"You know, I'm pretty sure there's something we can do," I said, "but I need to get in touch with my supervisor to find out how to go about it." Taking down the social worker's contact information, I promised I would get back to her soon.

Though not wholly familiar with all of Planned Parenthood's services, I knew the administrative office in Dallas had a teen sex education department. I had heard about the skits and plays that had been done at some of the more heavily populated sites to educate girls about birth control and safe sex. Perhaps someone there could help the girls at the detention facility.

When I reached my supervisor in the Dallas office, she explained that the worker who offered the program didn't travel outside the Dallas area. This seemed odd, given that twenty-some clinics were spread throughout the Dallas area, just an hour's drive from the city. Why institute all those locations without a plan to offer the services available to the main clinics? It wouldn't be until later that I would wonder whether those smaller clinics were being used primarily to send pregnant women to the abortion facilities where the bigger profits were made.

As my supervisor and I talked, even as the door threatened to shut, I gently resisted. Not willing to give up on those girls yet, I threw out a last-ditch suggestion. "I'm just wondering if this is something I could do?" I asked. "I mean, I'm certainly willing to get some training and give it a shot."

She told me that if I were willing to go to the Grayson facility on a day we didn't have clients scheduled, she would let me do it. She promised to e-mail me some links to materials that could help me to prepare.

That evening, I read up on the different educational techniques used to teach teens about making responsible sexual decisions. Though not trained as an educator, I felt up to giving it a try. Over the next several days I pored over the material to get ready for my presentation at the juvenile facility.

I still wanted very much to believe that Planned Parenthood existed to help people. Since we were all about prevention, I reasoned, if we could just get these young girls on birth control, we would be decreasing unwanted pregnancies, sexually transmitted diseases, and abortions. In the process, connecting the girls with our company could expand future clientele—something I knew would garner brownie points and perhaps a raise. When I called the social worker back, she was thrilled and promised she would give me a count of attendees soon.

A few weeks later, in the early afternoon, I left the Sherman facility after finishing paperwork at the office. The day was warm and sunny, and I felt a renewed sense of purpose as I drove onto the highway heading north into the country, toward the outskirts of Sherman.

The building where I was to conduct the sessions, a probation office, resembled an old schoolhouse. Just beyond it I could see the juvenile jail with its encircling barbed-wire fence.

As I made my way into the room where the session would take place, the girls began appearing one by one, some chatting and giggling, a few others alone and quiet. Two female probation officers came in with them and positioned themselves in opposite corners of the room.

I was struck by the innocent-looking faces of the girls, about a dozen of them, ages thirteen to seventeen. I knew that, under slightly different circumstances, I might have ended up in a place like this, or worse yet, Lorena might have.

Despite these discomforting thoughts, I felt an immediate sense of ease around the girls. Given where I was in life, including being the mother of one their age, I felt confident that I would be able to reach them. As I sifted through my materials, a maternal sense took over. I was overcome with wanting to nurture and to protect the girls who had willingly come to hear what I had to share.

With the help of some icebreakers, I began learning some of the particulars of their lives. One girl's protruding belly gave away part of her story. Another talked about her child, whom her mom was helping raise. All of them were living very risky lifestyles and had been in probation for one reason or another: some for truancy, others for things such as shoplifting. No hard-core criminals, but who knew what the future might hold if they stayed in their current environment without any tools to make a better way?

It was the perfect opportunity to do what I had always wanted to do: help young people by talking to them about sex education. At home, I had been teaching Lorena the importance of abstinence, and it seemed natural and right to do the same in this setting. But I felt conflicted. Would girls who were already sexually active, some with older men who acted like father figures, receive the information as well as Lorena had?

I presented the material starting with the basics, teaching first about the reproductive system and then moving on to birth control and STDs. We played several games, including one involving Wiffle balls. Some of the balls were plain, and others bore stickers representing different STDs. I tossed the balls to the girls, and they would look to see if they had gotten an STD or not. I shared statistics, such as the fact that one in three women will have an STD by the time she turns twenty-five, to give them a lasting impression of what they might expect if they continued along their current paths.

When they asked questions, I did my best to answer them, difficult as it was to face them, realizing what was at stake if they didn't follow through with what I was trying to impart.

As my time with the girls grew shorter, I began to feel a tug at my heart and sensed that I needed to stay until I had shared more than what had been in my notes. "These girls need to know they should stop doing what they're doing." I heard these words clearly in my head and knew I had to listen.

I turned more squarely toward the girls, shifting my tone slightly. "While this is all important," I began, "there's something else I want to share with you today." Feeling the stern gazes of the probation officers nearby, I continued, "I want you to know that God loves you very much, and more than anything else, he wants you to love yourselves."

I was off the page now, I realized, going into unplanned territory, not to mention taking a huge risk. But as I looked at the girls—particularly the young African American who had already experienced the pains of childbirth—I couldn't hold back.

"If I don't offer anything else to you today," I said, "I hope you will at least come away knowing that you deserve more than what life has given you so far."

Earlier, some of the girls had shared stories of being raised in broken homes, of rampant alcoholism, etc. Seeing pain, regret, and disappointment in their faces, I couldn't walk out without telling them how special they were. Since they seemed mostly attentive to what I was saying, possibly hearing this message of love for the very first time in their lives, I continued.

"You don't have to live this way. Just because you're not a virgin anymore doesn't mean you can't go back and be abstinent again. There is such a thing as a second virginity."

I then shared my own story about becoming a mom at seventeen and being in an abusive relationship before finding the courage to leave and eventually meeting a really good man. I wanted them to feel hopeful, to know they didn't have to settle for being bruised emotionally, physically, and spiritually.

I cautioned them that they were putting themselves at risk by having sex with older men, that despite what they might have been told by their boyfriends and others, birth control wouldn't guarantee a disease-free life.

Though I worried at first that I might be scaring them with the truth, eventually I drew courage from their faces. One girl even had tears dripping down her cheeks. I was reaching them.

"You're all beautiful", I said. "Yes, you're in here now, but there's hope."

The further I strayed from my outline, the more I sensed I was not operating alone. And in the midst of the discussion, I realized that birth control was not the solution to their problems at all and that if they didn't hear that from me, they might not hear it from anyone.

Finally, my time was up. I said good-bye and wished them well.

As I drove back to my clinic, I felt happy and heavyhearted at the same time: happy for having shared the truth and heavy with concern about how the girls' lives would turn out.

Had I gotten through? Would anyone in their lives affirm what I had said, tell them they matter? How many would just go back and do the same thing all over again?

As these questions arose in my mind, others quickly followed. Now that a crack of light had entered in, I couldn't stop them.

Ramona, what have you done at Planned Parenthood that has prevented one unwanted pregnancy? What are you really doing to prevent STDs? Are you promoting abstinence in a way that is at all effective?

The questions stirred doubts about the driving force behind the clinics, including my own. It certainly wasn't abstinence. There was no money at all to be made from that. As for contraceptives, often all they did was bring about a false sense of security.

The peace I had felt just a short while ago in speaking so forthrightly to those girls turned quickly into regret. Speaking the truth to them had created new questions in my mind that I had to answer.

What was the point of it all?

In my time so far at Planned Parenthood, I had crossed paths with hundreds of clients, the majority of whom I had met briefly and then sent on their way, a new supply of pills in hand. But it had been different with the girls of Grayson County. I had brought them into my world, as they had brought me into theirs, even if only for a few hours. I had invested in them by telling them about God and his love for them. I had given them, or at least had tried to give them, hope.

My original mission had been to convince the girls at Grayson County that they needed to be on birth control. But in talking to them, I had come to see that birth control wasn't a solution and was likely to send them back into the same dangerous situations, more vulnerable than ever.

What those girls needed most is what I had needed: the ultimate role model and father. They needed God. They needed to learn about loving themselves and being chaste and what that really means.

More than anything, I wanted to point them to Christ, because the only person who could save them was Jesus. But how could I do any of that while working for Planned Parenthood? Within those constraints, I had nothing to offer.

A few months later, the social worker tried to reach me again to invite me back. Wracked with confused emotions, I avoided her phone call. Seeing the slip of paper with a note asking to return her call as soon as possible, I ripped it up and threw it in the trash.

I couldn't go back, not if being there wouldn't make any difference. I had risked telling the truth once but wasn't so sure I would be able to do it again and keep my job. And if I went back and only gave them what I had been trained to teach, my presence would be a lie, and I couldn't do that to those girls. They deserved better. I just couldn't imagine facing them again now that this conflict growing quietly within my heart had popped to the surface.

Along with a growing resentment toward Planned Parenthood and its limitations, I felt a troubling sense of culpability. I had been going overboard to prove what a great manager I was, that I could make money and still care about the people we were serving, but for what end? Could I honestly say we cared about our clients at Planned Parenthood? The only thing that felt certain now was that my future seemed more uncertain than ever.

10

The Flip of a Dial

"I'm going to stop by Walmart on the way home tonight to price bikes for the girls", I told Eugene by phone one afternoon. "Could you pick up a pizza for the kids in case I'm a little late?"

It was a Wednesday evening in December 2010, and in anticipation of our holiday bonus, I thought I would steal away to do some Christmas shopping. We wanted to buy Lorena and Savannah, now teenagers, some new bikes so that they could ride around town together when Savannah would come up from her mother's for the weekend. But on the drive to Walmart, my mind was filled with thoughts that had nothing to do with new bicycles.

A few things were at play. For one, an interim CEO at our company had been throwing us all for a loop with a slew of new changes and requirements. In addition to that, I was concerned about something that had happened to Linda.

After being accepted into a phlebotomy program at a local university, Linda had learned of the reversal of that decision, which would prevent her from continuing her studies. She was such a hard worker with so much to offer, and I wanted nothing more than to see her achieve her dreams. It seemed clear that she had been wronged, and the injustice felt like one more thing that I couldn't control or change.

All this tumbled through my mind as I arrived at the store and looked for a parking spot. As I slowly circled the lot, my hand reached for the radio and began searching, as if I were looking to hear something that would provide a solution to the problems in my life.

I had discovered Catholic radio several years earlier, though at that time I wasn't too interested in listening further. We had had an electricity outage in our neighborhood, and when I got home from work, my clock radio had reverted to the AM band and to a Catholic station I hadn't known existed. Before turning the dial to get back to my favorite FM tunes, I caught part of an interview with a young woman named Lila Rose.

Hearing her name stopped me for a moment because it had come up at the office. Because of Lila's undercover journalism work with Live Action, an organization she founded, she had been looked upon as a potential threat to our company, though I hadn't paid much attention to the particulars since it didn't seem to affect our little office.

During the radio interview, Lila talked about growing up in a large home as one of seven kids. I couldn't help but roll my eyes in disgust. *Whatever! Not everyone can afford a big family like that. Who does this woman think she is, anyway?* I quickly got back onto the FM band, glad to hear a familiar tune. And yet something Lila had said, or the way she had said it, lingered in my subconscious mind.

By that December evening in the Walmart parking lot, I was in a different place. I did want to know more. Increasingly disillusioned at work, I had begun craving another perspective. I couldn't yet name it, but I felt something was missing from Planned Parenthood's worldview.

I was beyond thinking that any Christian interpretation of life would do. I felt for some reason that I needed the Catholic one. As much as I had discounted the small bit about Lila I had heard previously, it had bugged me just enough to leave me questioning what the truth really was.

For someone as bullheaded as I, who needed to be right at all costs— the girl who would end up in verbal combat in personal encounters— Catholic radio presented a safe way for me to search for answers to the questions tapping at my conscience.

For some time, I had been experiencing an unrelenting, secret turmoil. My interior desire of wanting to do the right thing seemed in continual conflict with my exterior life. As in my childhood, I felt like someone engaged in an intense game of tug-of-war.

At work, "every child should be a wanted child" was the constant message. We were reminded of this both overtly and covertly through the thinking of our company's founder, Margaret Sanger. This idea that every child should be planned, or not exist at all, provided the basis for what we did each day.

But something about that mantra wasn't ringing true. New pushes at work to pack more and more clients into each day, and without additional resources, seemed to contradict our verbalized commitment to those we served.

As I searched for a parking space, I flipped through the FM stations, hoping to find an interesting talk show that might provide some answers to my abyss of questions. When nothing turned up, I did something unusual and switched to the AM band. As the dial landed on 910 AM my fingers froze.

Being featured that December night on Guadalupe Radio was a two-hour Catholic Answers show on abortion. The host had announced that the first hour would primarily involve taking calls from Catholic women who had had abortions. I let go of the dial and listened.

One of the guests had gotten pregnant at age twelve after being raped by a family member. Through tears she talked about how her mother, to protect the family secret, had forced her to get an abortion. Since abortion was illegal at the time, the family had gone through extraordinary measures to kill the child. The woman spoke of her feelings of powerlessness and of how long it had taken her to get over not only the rape but the abortion on top of it. If she had had a choice, she said, she would have had the baby.

I was stunned. The story went against everything we had been led to believe was right. She was young and a rape victim. From the perspective of Planned Parenthood, this was the perfect candidate for abortion. And yet here she was, saying otherwise. Had it been a choice for her? It didn't seem so.

I shivered and turned up the volume a few notches as the next guest took her turn. After describing the details leading up to her abortion, the speaker talked about the experience itself. "We were treated like cattle," she began, "herded about like animals, nobody really reaching out in love or giving us time to think about our options. It seemed clear they just wanted to get us in and out as quickly as possible."

Hearing her talk, I felt my heart jump. Her story seemed to match my experiences as a staff member feeling pressured to push the clients through, hearing all the cautionary notes about low numbers and the need to work harder to reverse that. Deep inside, I had questioned the way we were treating our clients, and now here was this woman—the kind of woman we served and supposedly cared for—validating my concerns.

In recent months, our clinic with three staff members had been seeing as many patients as some of the bigger clinics. Lacking support to carry out our work successfully, I had been doing everything possible to get my supervisor to see that our schedule simply couldn't accommodate the insisted-upon outcome. More often than not, we had to make clients wait two or three hours to be seen, and no one seemed to bat an eye. To me, this practice did not match our mission.

Because I wanted to provide personal care in my clinic but found it impossible to do so most of the time, I shifted uncomfortably in my seat as the woman on the radio described the dehumanizing treatment she had received. We didn't do abortions at our contraception-only clinic, but our mindset was the same as that of the abortion provider. In spite of my good intentions, I was becoming a cattle herder too.

Looking at the clock, I knew I should get inside the store, but before the break the host mentioned that the second half of the show would contain a segment on contraception, and I couldn't force myself to move.

The guest on that segment was a priest, and in the discussion, he mentioned a word I had never heard before—*abortifacient*. I learned, for the first time, that some contraceptives have the capacity to abort a new life without the mother's knowing it. I flashed through my memories. *What if I, through my own contraceptive use, had unintentionally aborted one of my own children?*

There was a time in my first marriage, a few years after Lorena was born, when I was using a hormone patch to prevent pregnancy and had experienced some horrendous cramping. I still remember the odd blood clot in the toilet that looked more like irregularly shaped pink tissue. Had it been a tiny child?

It had long been bothering me, this issue of contraception. I knew that the Church was against it, but I had discounted that, hoping some-how it was the one area in which the Church was wrong. After all, I worked in a place that existed for this purpose.

Planned Parenthood had recently alerted its managers that the com-pany wanted us to be trained to draw blood and to administer Depo-Provera shots. The memo deeply bothered me. I really felt this kind of change should require more than a few hours of on-the-job training, and it wasn't something I had signed up for.

I had been doing a pretty good job of getting around those aspects of my job that bothered me, but this was coming a little too close to my moral compass. When the priest on the radio specifically mentioned Depo-Provera and its higher potential of being an abortifacient, a sink-ing feeling came over me. How would I get around this one?

It was beginning to make sense to me why the Church teaches against contraception. For years, I had been justifying my work with the thought that I was not directly associated with abortion, but this new information was a game changer. By dispensing contraception, I was not only potentially dispensing harmful drugs and devices, but possibly helping to destroy new life.

When the next break came on, I realized how much time had passed. I needed to get moving, or Eugene would worry. I was on information overload, anyway, completely overwhelmed. Yet I thought that I had just stumbled upon something significant.

I hurried into Walmart and headed directly for the shiny bicycles. As I searched the tags, looking for the best deal, a heavy feeling came over me. Shopping for new bikes for our girls normally would be a joyous occasion, but joy was the last emotion I was experiencing that December evening.

Later I would see this day as pivotal. I had been feeling tossed about for a while, one minute feeling I was in the right place and the next feeling angry but not knowing exactly why. Didn't every job come with its share of requirements that stink? But you suck it up like everyone else and do what's required to get the paycheck, right?

This time, however, the issue was beyond short lunch breaks and being understaffed. On so many days I had come home from work upset. "I've had it with this place", I would tell Eugene. He would ask why, and I couldn't come up with a solid reason—not one big enough to merit my leaving. I had never before stumbled upon something that would compromise my moral convictions so directly.

It was as if God had been slowly revealing the truth to me. Or maybe he had always revealed it, but I was finally at the right place to receive it. There in the Walmart parking lot, God was setting it up for me, saying, "Okay, now that I've got your attention, I'm going to expose you to some truths. In time, it will all make sense."

He knew that it wouldn't be long before the chips would fall into place and in a way that would allow me to interpret them rightly. But they had to fall one by one for me to see.

The only hope I felt as I headed back to Trenton that night was what had come from 910 AM, Guadalupe Radio. Maybe if I kept listening, I would find clues or answers or perhaps even learn something to convince me that what I was doing at Planned Parenthood was just fine. I was open to wherever my discoveries might lead.

And so I continued to listen to Catholic radio on that drive to and from work, three days a week, absorbing, searching, and hoping to land on God's will once and for all.

* * * * *

In January, while on my drive to work, I caught the tail end of a radio interview with a guest who had been introduced as Abby Johnson, a former Planned Parenthood director and author of a new book. Just as this was being announced, I pulled into the clinic parking lot. Reluctantly I turned off my car and headed inside.

Later that day, during a lull, I looked up on my computer the title of the book, *Unplanned*. I'll have to get a copy sometime, I thought, filing the information away in my mind for some future time—a time when knowing Abby's story would become even more relevant.

* * * * *

Christmas that year turned out to be one of the worst of my life. I had always anticipated with excitement the time when Christ's birth would be celebrated. But our family had been undergoing some extremely challenging moments. Mainly, I was concerned over the strained relationship Eugene was having with Savannah. The two had gotten into a horrible argument, and it seemed as if their relationship was coming apart at the seams, affecting all of us.

One morning, finding no other way to deal with this, I got up early and began sprinkling holy water around the house, praying for the graces of God to kick in. I worried about our family's ability to persevere, and I felt the great heaviness of a life in disarray.

Later I would interpret this time of unrest as a spiritual battle, with my soul as the prize for the victor. In a way, though, it also seems that God was preparing me, helping me to empty myself of anything that might prevent me from hearing him as clearly as possible. By being bent at the knees, I would more easily be able to receive the truths necessary to move through the next steps.

Through Catholic radio, I continued to learn more about my faith and the pro-life movement. I listened intently for contradictions that would allow me to continue justifying my work. But none surfaced. Instead, the teachings and ideas were cohesive and whole and, as I was finding, refreshingly illuminating.

The ambiguity with which I had been living was slowly pulling me in the direction of light, and it felt good. I had never wanted to denounce my faith, after all. As a child and as an adult, I was happy to claim my Catholic identity. I had felt at home in the Church. It had been only in recent years, since working for Planned Parenthood, really, that I had had to profess this under my breath, afraid that I would be questioned or found unworthy.

The more the truths I was discovering through Catholic radio took hold, the more my faith in Planned Parenthood diminished.

11

The Videotape

I first heard the name Lila Rose in 2008, when I received notification at work about a college student who had been posing as an underage girl seeking an abortion. We had been told to post her picture on our bulletin board so that we would recognize her if she came into our clinic. I did as I was told and went on with my business.

Eventually I learned Lila's history, including the beginnings of the pro-life club she had founded as a teen in 2003 to draw together other young pro-lifers to discourage abortion. In 2008 the club legally became a nonpartisan, nonprofit organization called Live Action. As its website states, the organization uses investigative journalism to educate people about abortion.

Lila's name resurfaced in our clinic in February 2011, when we were called to attend a company-wide training session. We were told the meeting would involve managers to discuss a video that had been released recently by Live Action. The footage had been captured by undercover Live Action members posing as people involved in sex-trafficking.

Despite a hushed buzz over the video, I really didn't understand what the fuss was about. After all, I was in a small clinic in Sherman, not in one of the larger sites that would be more directly impacted. Nevertheless, our affiliate wanted everyone on board.

After the initial e-mail, follow-up memos came with more details about the trainings that would take place in various locations, including North Texas. Why had this Lila Rose captured the attention of our company head more than once, I wondered quietly. Despite my questions, I was still more irritated than anything else, and I didn't really feel up to attending a meeting an hour away from home when other, more important work needed to be done at the office.

After reading the final memo, I walked over to where Linda was filing some papers. "How can they expect us to get all this work done if we're supposed to attend a meeting an hour away that more than likely doesn't affect us?" I asked her.

"Tell me about it", Linda said. "What are the chances we can talk them into overtime for this little adventure?"

"How about zero to none?" I said, rolling my eyes.

There was nothing more to do but to start making arrangements for the day to come. Although my allegiance to my employer was now questionable in my mind, my motivations were, at that point, still fairly selfish. I was more concerned about wasting gas on the drive to and from Gainesville, where the meeting would take place, than anything else.

On the morning of the meeting, my mood was apathetic at best. I was convinced nothing new could come forward that would change my mind about my growing unease with Planned Parenthood. Feeling unmotivated, I dawdled while getting ready for the day.

The Gainesville site was a small house in the middle of a residential neighborhood. Signing in at the entry, I realized I was the last to arrive. I quickly found my way to the room where the meeting was taking place, hoping to be as unobtrusive as possible.

"Uh, sorry I'm late", I mumbled. I scanned the dimly lit room for Linda and then slipped into the chair closest to the door, a bit out of breath. Sizing up the group, I noted about twelve employees representing three clinics.

"Okay, we're all here now. Let's get started", said Jean, the director of nurses from the administrative office in Dallas who would lead the meeting. Our area manager, Julie, sat near Jean.

We were shown a video with fuzzy images captured by the undercover camera of a man seeking assistance for procuring abortions, testing for sexually transmitted diseases, and obtaining birth control for girls he confessed to be "managing" as sex workers. He described the girls as being from out of the country and as young as fourteen or fifteen. The clinic worker assured him the conversation would be confidential and assisted the man without question, despite the illegal action he was revealing.

As the footage continued, I sensed some of the women around me fidgeting. The more my eyes adjusted to the darkened room, the more easily I could discern the obviously confused looks on many of their faces. A few were expressionless.

Surely this is going somewhere, I thought. It's just a matter of time before Jean will cut in and explain how all of this relates explicitly to our work at our clinics.

A variety of other videos followed, each showing similar undercover operations at various sites. One revealed callers offering to donate money specifically to abort minority babies. The filmed Planned Parenthood employee asked few questions and assured the callers that the money would be used as requested.

As the video played, Jean looked around the room, as if trying to read our reactions. Julie seemed unusually quiet, as if reluctant to say anything in Jean's presence. I kept looking at Linda, wondering what she was thinking. Even though I still doubted this kind of thing would ever happen at our clinic, I was growing more curious as to what the advice to us would be.

But Jean never said anything about how we could help our clients. Instead, she started a PowerPoint presentation offering tips on what to do in the event Live Action were to target one of our clinics, ideas on how to protect ourselves from such an intrusion.

I doodled in a notebook to release the tension over what was unfolding. Finally, feeling the need to break the silence from the workers in attendance, I spoke up. What did I have to lose?

"Jean, uh, I guess what I'm wondering is, what will we do as managers if something like this really does happen at our clinics?" I asked. "How can we be prepared so that if it does happen, we can make sure our clients are safe and nothing illegal is going on?"

An awkward silence followed, and then Jean, clearly taken aback, responded in a stern voice, "We're not here to discuss that, Ramona. We're here to identify whether we're being violated by an undercover operation."

No one else said anything, though I felt more approval in the quiet than not, as if most of the others were thinking along the same lines as I was.

"There are ways to identify whether we are being recorded on the phone or Internet, and that's what we're here to learn", Jean emphasized.

Throughout the rest of the meeting, my stomach churned. The unease that had accompanied me into the meeting had been bumped up a few notches.

Jean sent us home with a pile of papers, mainly memos concerning what to look for in identifying potential undercover operations, including certain phrases that might be used to tip us off.

Afterward, I met Linda on the sidewalk out front.

"So what did you think?" she asked.

"Something smells funny", I said in a near whisper. "I need to process this a little more, but let's talk back at the office, okay?"

On the drive back, my mind was awhirl. By the time I reached the office, I was eager to talk with Linda. Thankfully, it was a nonclient day.

"This is it, Linda. I'm disgusted with this place. I thought the meeting was going to be about recognizing abuse", I said.

"I know, I know", Linda said, shaking her head. "I can't believe it either. What are they thinking?"

"I don't know," I said, "but I can't help but wonder if there's something we're not being told."

Locking up for the evening, I felt a surge of relief as I pulled the door shut. I couldn't wait to get in the car, blast the radio all the way back to Trenton, and just zone out for a while.

12

A Lent to Remember

Easter was by far the most celebrated holiday of the year within our extended family when I was growing up. Because my grandparents owned a nice piece of land large enough to accommodate all of us, each spring they would invite our large brood—cousins, uncles, aunts, and everyone in between—over to their place for a huge fiesta.

Most of the day would be spent preparing for or indulging in a barbecue feast and an Easter egg hunt for the kids. The party would continue into the evening, at least until the sun had set and we could no longer see the expressions of happiness on one another's faces. It was an absolute, joy-filled blast, and many of my favorite childhood memories were fashioned during these gatherings.

I wouldn't characterize any of us back then as devout Catholics. Some would use the phrase *cultural Catholics* to describe how we lived out our faith. We all had been baptized, and we embraced certain customs and traditions of the Church. But we were not necessarily well catechized. Certain Catholic customs and seasons, however, were as infused into our lives as certain elements of our Mexican heritage—remnants from the old days.

Though attending Sunday Mass was hit or miss for most of us, we would be in Church every Ash Wednesday without fail. This day launched the beginning of Lent, after all, and Lent served as the preview to the main event of Easter, which would bring us all together once again. We knew the day deserved our devotion.

We took Lent very seriously, including no-meat Friday meals. My grandma would go even further, abstaining from meat every day during Lent. The rest of us made smaller sacrifices, giving up at least one of our favorite indulgences. One year, my father even gave up drinking for those forty days. In this way, Lent became a hopeful thing to me, a glimpse of the good life that was possible.

Upon being confirmed in 2005, Eugene and I were committed to growing in faith, starting with regular Mass attendance. We did pretty well with this until three years into it, around the time I started at Planned Parenthood. Life by then had become so busy that we began finding excuses not to get up early enough on Sunday mornings to make it to Mass.

But as soon as Ash Wednesday rolled around, we were first in line to receive the ashes, that important reminder to me of my imperfect nature and, thus, my need for God. Without complaint or question, we willingly continued to give up small luxuries such as soda and sweets in order to embrace the season.

* * * * *

Before Ash Wednesday 2011, I had been listening to Catholic radio for several months, and I was becoming better formed in my faith as a result. Having heard so many talk programs and faith discussions on my drives to and from work, I had a growing desire to make my next Lent more meaningful than the last one. As neither Eugene nor I had been to reconciliation since right before our wedding, a good place to start, I thought, was the confessional.

I also wanted to add something new to my daily Lenten routine to keep me focused on fasting, prayer, and almsgiving. Because I had such fond memories of my grandmother's reciting the Rosary in my earliest years, I decided I would pray a daily Rosary and read one Scripture passage each day of Lent. But first, I wanted to confess my sins to a priest in order to have the best fresh start possible and to clear my conscience.

As I walked through the parking lot of Saint Michael the Archangel Church, our home parish in McKinney, my heart began to pound. I pulled open the large exterior doors and wondered if I would remember the order of everything. I was nervous but excited.

O my God, I am heartily sorry for having offended you ...

As I practiced the words of the Act of Contrition and waited for my turn in the confessional, my heart raced. "Dear God, help me to make a good confession", I prayed quietly in the pew. "I want to go all out, and if that means mentioning that I use contraception and where I work, well, I want to bring that to light. I think I'm ready, God, but please help me. I'm a little scared."

Father Cruz was a very young, vibrant priest, perhaps in his early thirties. Although he was Mexican, and Spanish was his native language, I felt more comfortable confessing in English, my native tongue. He very gently led me through everything and, at the end of it all, said I had made a great confession. I sighed deeply, with a smile of gratitude on my face.

I had put everything out there. I had said the words and, through that, had faced the wrongs in my life. To my delight, rather than falling into a hole because of it, I had been offered forgiveness. What a wonderful feeling.

After absolving me from all my sins, but before the dismissal, Father Cruz paused a moment. Then he said he had a few more things he wanted to say before I left to do my penance.

First, he congratulated me for my good confession and my decision to quit taking contraceptives, which I had decided just a few days before. Father Cruz then encouraged me to consider Natural Family Planning as a way to space our children. His words were just what I needed to continue down the right path.

But then he delivered the bombshell.

"This isn't going to be easy, and it might not happen right away", he began. I folded my hands and pressed my thumbs into my palms as a way to prepare physically for what might come next.

"But it's important for you to realize that the place where you work and spend so much of your time is also contrary to the will of God. In fact, by working there, you're putting your soul in danger."

Despite the directness in his words, hearing them gave me almost as much relief as hearing the absolution. They were not words of condemnation, but of love, gentleness, and compassion. And his voice confirmed to me that I was no longer alone in grappling with the thoughts inside my head, the constant deliberation over whether I was doing something wrong by both using and distributing contraception. I was grateful for his guidance, and I knew that it meant I really would have to leave Planned Parenthood.

I walked out with tears trickling down my face and paused to inhale the fresh air. It really was as if the weight of the world had been lifted from my shoulders.

Yes, there was work to do, and I didn't know how it would all come to pass. But I sensed that in time the answers would come and that I would not be alone. I slowly began walking, and with each step I felt more hopeful and assured that sometime during this season of repentance and new beginnings, clearer answers would emerge.

* * * * *

To kick off Lent 2011, my family and I attended an evening Ash Wednesday service, which gave me an opportunity to reflect on an idea I had been tossing around in my head.

I had grown up hearing the Rosary recited at funerals and other Catholic celebrations, and at some point I had picked up a little Rosary guide to help me work my way through the prayers and the meditations. During some of my lowest moments as a young mother, the Rosary had been a comfort to me, but it had remained a prayer I said only occasionally.

With so many realizations coming to light, about things that seemed bigger than what I could handle alone, I sensed the need to beef up my Lenten commitment; and the Rosary seemed like a good way to arm myself with the spiritual reserves I would need. By the time we left Mass, my ashen cross in place on my forehead, I was resolute: instead of giving up something for Lent, as I had done all the years before, I would add a daily Rosary.

That night and the thirty-nine others that followed, I said my Lenten Rosary, lying in bed and running my fingers over the beads while nestled warmly under the covers. Some nights, Elijah, now four, would cuddle next to me and attempt his own versions of the Hail Mary and Glory Be, which were becoming familiar to his ears. I loved having him there, his big brown eyes looking into mine, and hearing his sweet voice praying alongside me. Though he frequently interrupted with questions, I would just smile at him and keep on praying, allowing the calming power of the Rosary to penetrate my being, body and soul.

Most nights, this regimen had me falling asleep easily and peacefully. But one night, I felt more alert than sleepy. A couple of days into my Rosary routine—one short week after that fateful confession and day three into the 40 Days for Life campaign outside my clinic—I was sitting on the edge of my bed with my beads in hand, and I could feel my heart and soul beginning to fuse together. I began to cry. The gentle voice I had come to recognize as the Holy Spirit's breathed into me, "You're close now. It's nearing the time to start a new chapter."

Thankfully, Elijah hadn't crawled under the covers with me that night, because I likely would have held back to avoid scaring him. Instead, he had fallen asleep in his own bed, leaving me alone with the loving, comforting presence of God, who, I was sure now, would give me the strength I would need for whatever was next.

* * * * *

Since February, I had been hearing ads on Catholic radio from an obstetrician-gynecologist in Dallas who embraced only pro-life principles and practices. This was something of an epiphany, and I pondered why someone would take such a brave stance, risking an abundant livelihood by going against the grain. One day I even pulled the car to the side of the road so that I could write down his name, hoping I would be brave enough someday to give him a call.

Ever since my confession to Father Cruz, I no longer doubted that using contraception was harmful, and I was becoming more intrigued by the thought of spacing children naturally without using chemicals that mess with the natural hormonal input and output. One day, feeling ready to put all of this inspiration into practice, I called Dr. Joseph Behan and scheduled an appointment. Soon, my dependence on contraception, both emotionally and physically, would be over.

To apply Father Cruz's words to my job, however, required a greater effort; but each decade of the Rosary was creating within me the courage I needed to part from Planned Parenthood.

Hail Mary, full of grace, the Lord is with thee.

The 40 Days for Life group outside my clinic was also praying for me to have courage. I recalled the prayer circle at Nancy's former clinic and was struck that while this was apparently becoming a national effort, it had started right here in Texas, not all that far from my home.

A year earlier, I would have been disturbed at the thought of these prayer circles widening. It would have bugged me that these people would show up at our clinic of all places—a clinic, like Nancy's, that didn't even perform abortions. But by now, I welcomed their presence, because I was beginning to feel that those protestors may well be a key to my escape. They had been kind to Nancy, after all. Maybe this would be my chance to ask for prayer or to get some kind of support by talking to an actual pro-lifer. They were not the enemy. I was sure of that now.

Among the 40 Days for Life group outside the Sherman clinic was a man who had been praying there for some time, before this particular campaign began. I had noticed that he would show up to pray, rain or shine. His face seemed kind, like a grandfather's, and I had wondered what would compel him to come out even in bad weather. Soon enough I would meet some of the other prayer people and learn just what drove them there.

* * * * *

The Friday after Ash Wednesday, as I looked out the front window of the clinic, watching the prayer circle form, I recalled one of the last conversations I had with Nancy before she left Planned Parenthood.

"Ramona, I'll be praying for you, okay?" she had said. "I hope that someday you'll leave, too." She had told me that there were more openings at the children's hospital that had hired her and that she could help me find an in.

"I'm not really ready yet", I had said. "I'm just not ready for full time." Despite my growing misgivings, I was still feeling secure with my three days a week of work and my pleasant commute. I had not wanted to mess with that just yet.

Since that conversation, I had been wondering why Nancy had said she was praying for me. She had sounded worried about me, but I didn't understand why, and I wasn't even sure I wanted to know. The answer might be something that would force me out of my comfort zone.

After only two evenings of praying the Lenten Rosary, however, I was seeing things I hadn't seen before, including the link between Planned Parenthood and abortion. I was beginning to understand why the protesters would rearrange their lives to pray at the clinic even in inclement weather. Only something as big as life and death could be a strong enough reason for people to disrupt their busy routines to go somewhere just to pray.

I had been a people pleaser all of my life, and in recent years, I had been trying valiantly to please my employer. But as I peered out at the people gathered at the edge of the parking lot, clinging to their signs and prayers, questions formed in my mind.

What am I doing here?

Planned Parenthood is keeping our family fed, I answered myself.

But at what cost?

I had committed to working part time at the Sherman clinic only until Elijah was potty-trained, and I had been poking around for a full-time job ever since we had passed that milestone some months ago. Since crossing the threshold of Lent, the search had taken on greater urgency, and I had been wondering whether the people praying outside the clinic might be able to help me.

I went into one of the rooms in back and paused for a few moments. Closing my eyes, I began praying. "God, I think this is the day. Help me to have the courage to talk to them. Give me the words."

After locking up, I walked to the parking lot. A woman standing outside waved to me, and after waving back, I quickly got into my car. My chance to talk to her had passed; I had chickened out.

Driving away, I realized I had forgotten the deposit.

"Dang", I said, and I pulled into a strip mall parking lot in order to circle back to the clinic.

When I returned, I noticed the same woman I had seen before. After retrieving the deposit, I headed out to my car again, but this time I stopped, my heart thumping madly.

This is it, Mona. This is your chance. Don't blow it.

Feeling safe enough, I walked over to her.

"Hi," I said, "I'm Ramona."

I could tell she was startled.

"Well, hi, sweetie", she said. "My name is Lynn. It's a pleasure to meet you."

As it turned out, she wasn't even supposed to be there. She wasn't part of the 40 Days for Life effort at all. But finding her kind and welcoming, I told her I was an employee of the clinic.

"Do you think abortion is okay?" she finally asked me.

"Of course not."

"Well, by working under the label of Planned Parenthood, you are implicitly involved in abortion."

I decided I needed to be forthcoming and to tell her I was manager of the clinic.

"Oh my", she said. "Well, hon, in that case, I'm wondering if you wouldn't mind if we said a little prayer together. Would that be okay?"

"Sure", I said, pleased that she had asked.

After the prayer, I told her that I had been conflicted for a while about working there and that I was considering getting out. She gave me a big hug and said, "God bless you, dear. You know, the Lord provides a way for those who follow his heart."

"Thanks," I said, "thanks for saying that."

As we talked, a pickup pulled into the parking lot, and a man got out. After a few moments, he approached us, introducing himself as Gerry Brundage. He explained that he had organized the Sherman 40 Days for Life prayer group, and within minutes, he was sharing his perspective of the abortion industry as a practicing Catholic.

"Have you ever heard of Abby Johnson?" he finally asked.

I said that I had and thought back to the short introduction I had heard on Catholic radio and my curiosity about her story.

"Just a minute," Gerry said, "I have to go get something from my pickup." A few moments later, he was back with a copy of Abby's *Unplanned* in his hands, saying, "You need to read Abby's story."

I thanked him and said that I would return it to him soon.

"Oh, don't worry too much about it", he said, smiling. "We'll be out here until right before Easter, so there's plenty of time."

Before we parted, I mentioned that my coworker had been looking around for another job too. Gerry and I exchanged phone numbers and e-mail addresses and parted ways.

By the following Tuesday, Gerry had already e-mailed me, saying that if I sent him my résumé, he would do everything possible to help me and Linda to find work outside of Planned Parenthood.

The life-changing move was now imminent. It was just a matter now of details, how specifically it would all unfold.

13

Divine Mercy

Despite the spiritual awakening that Lent had set in motion, Easter 2011 seemed to pass by without my noticing. It was as if the Resurrection of Christ had taken a backseat to the intensification of my own personal drama.

When I look back, the fog makes sense. After all, it was during this Lent that I had pulled into our driveway after work and been hit with Barbara McGuigan's stark question—the one that had sent my soul spinning.

The query "What did you do?" had become a haunting refrain, reminding me nearly every hour of the day that if I didn't turn things around, and quickly, I would sink more deeply into sin.

Change was needed, there was no doubt, but I felt stymied by the variables, especially the possible implications of leaving my job. Yes, it was a job that had put my soul in danger, but wouldn't walking away from it compromise my family to the point of making things even worse? No matter how I looked at things, I just couldn't see a way out.

When Good Friday arrived, I was determined to experience it as never before. I had heard about a Stations of the Cross dramatization to be presented at our parish and wanted more than anything to attend. Eugene's employer had always given him the day off for religious observance, as had past employers of mine. Planned Parenthood was the first not to make it an automatic holiday, and I felt anxious about whether they would give me a pass. In the end, I did get the day off and convinced my whole family to accompany me to the Stations.

The dramatization proved deeply moving. Watching the scene of Jesus' death, portrayed with such authentic emotions by the actors, I felt as if I were right there with him. As I heard his final words, "Father, into your hands I commend my spirit", tears trickled down my cheeks. The shift within was taking hold with each step toward Christ's last breath.

And that's where I rested for the next week—in the place of Jesus' death and what had been done to him. My strong identification with that moment of confusion and sadness was necessary, but it also made me feel more panicked about the crucifixion I might be facing. In light of these thoughts, my Easter joy had necessarily become muted.

The first Sunday after Easter, May 1, stands out in dramatic detail, however, for that's the day I jumped into the deep unknown and, on the descent, grabbed hold of the only thing that could save me.

* * * * *

As Eugene led Lorena and me, with Elijah on my hip, through the doors of Saint Michael's Church, I dipped my free hand into the font at the church's entrance and traced a cross on my forehead with cool holy water. After a bit of the usual rustling, we settled into a pew near the back.

Elijah wriggled behind me as I knelt to pray, "Lord, thank you for bringing me here. I'm ready to hear whatever it is you want to tell me."

The first reading of that Divine Mercy Sunday went by in a blur while I did my best to keep Elijah still. But when the lector started the second reading, all motion around me stopped as the words began winding their way into my heart.

> Blessed be the God and Father of our Lord Jesus Christ, who in his great mercy gave us a new birth to a living hope through the resurrection of Jesus Christ from the dead, to an inheritance that is imperishable, undefiled, and unfading, kept in heaven for you who by the power of God are safeguarded through faith, to a salvation that is ready to be revealed in the final time. In this you rejoice, although now for a little while you may have to suffer through various trials, so that the genuineness of your faith, more precious than gold that is perishable even though tested by fire, may prove to be for praise, glory, and honor at the revelation of Jesus Christ. Although you have not seen him you love him; even though you do not see him now yet believe in him, you rejoice with an indescribable and glorious joy, as you attain the goal of your faith, the salvation of your souls. (1 Pet 1:3–9)

Hearing these words, I felt overwhelmed with joy and hope, and tears began welling up in my eyes. God seemed to be saying that even though it would be hard to leave my job, and I would go through some suffering in the process, I still needed to do it and to trust. Yes, my soul had been in danger up to that point, but I was beginning to see that God's mercy would carry me through to whatever was next.

Though I felt a sense of urgency, this was coupled by an even stronger feeling of serenity and peace. The fears I had been carrying began to melt away with the assurance of God's loving protection.

Little did I know that the reading was only the prelude to what was about to happen. During Communion, God touched me in a way I had never before experienced; it was really the hymn that did me in.

> Lord, when you came to the seashore, you weren't seeking the wise or the wealthy, but only asking that I might follow.

That's me, isn't it, Lord?

> O Lord, in my eyes you were gazing, kindly smiling, my name you were saying; All I treasured, I have left on the sand there; close to you, I will find other seas.

I will find other seas.

> Lord, you knew what my boat carried: neither money nor weapons for fighting, but nets for fishing, my daily labor.
> Lord, have you need of my labor, hands for service, a heart made for loving, my arms for lifting the poor and broken?
> Lord, send me where you would have me, to a village, or heart of the city; I will remember that you are with me.
> O Lord, in my eyes you were gazing, kindly smiling, my name you were saying; All I treasured, I have left on the sand there; close to you, I will find other seas.

I felt the Lord comforting me, saying, "I forgive you. Believe in me; have faith in me." I was wrapped completely in his merciful love as he spoke to me through the words of the song, showing me my future.

I felt hope regarding the good things to come, though I couldn't possibly know what they would be exactly. It was like being pregnant, knowing almost nothing about the new life within me yet sensing what that life might become and trusting in a good outcome.

Later I would learn more about the special graces of that day, Divine Mercy Sunday, the feast instituted by Pope John Paul II to celebrate the vision of God's mercy experienced by Saint Faustina Kowalska. I would read how Jesus had inspired this Polish nun to pray ardently for his mercy and to have complete trust in him.

Even though I didn't yet understand how this Sunday after Easter had been set aside for Divine Mercy, I felt God giving me this tremendous gift of his love. I looked at Eugene, tears in my eyes, and he looked back in a way that told me he, too, knew something powerful was taking place. Even Lorena, now sixteen, squeezed my hand to offer quiet comfort.

Though we all sensed then just how significant this time was for me and my spiritual journey, from the outside it would not make sense why that song had penetrated my heart so deeply. Sure, it was a beautiful song, but why the breakdown? It would take time for me to comprehend fully all that was at work, all that had led up to that moment.

It had been only days before, after all, that I had experienced that jolting revelation in the driveway, with God's convicting words spoken to me through a radio host.

For a while I had been seeing the wrongness of how I had been living my life and on what I had been basing my actions. But I had not, until just days before, comprehended fully how I had been participating in evil through writing abortion referrals and handing out contraceptives. With terror, I had confronted the implications for my own soul and had realized that there was no way through it but out, and yet such a move seemed impossible.

Convinced I had to get out but feeling I could not had paralyzed me, but when the words of that song touched my ears that morning at Mass, the fear in which I had been frozen for days began to melt and to be replaced by an indescribable surge of relief.

In the driveway, Jesus had said, "You need to see this, and it's going to be very hard; but in a few days I'm going to show you the way out." This time he said, "Trust in me. I will lead you over. You are completely safe in my arms."

At Mass that Divine Mercy Sunday, everything collided—the referrals, the scared looks on young people's faces and my feelings of helplessness, the avoidance of the truth because I could not face the consequences, and finally, the recognition of the blood on my own hands. But all this was met with the glad realization that I did not have to remain in that place—that God would lead me to other, more blessed shores if I would let go and let him guide me.

So many times I had said, "It's not my place to judge. It's not my problem. It doesn't affect me." Now I fully understood that I would be held accountable for whatever ways I had led others away from truth and love, but also, that God would cradle me in his arms if I let go and left my old life behind.

As the Holy Spirit washed over me like waves lapping on the shores of my heart, there was no denying it—God had been leading me, step-by-step, to this moment of mercy. Only later would I see, in the image of Jesus with his overflowing heart and the words "Jesus, I trust in you", that our experiences on Divine Mercy Sunday were even more significant than any of us could have known that day.

On the way home from Mass, one thing was abundantly clear: God was asking me to go forward in faith and trust.

* * * * *

Lauren Muzyka, an attorney and campaign strategist for 40 Days for Life National, had come into my life a week before that Sunday.

Later she would tell me how she had been deep in prayer over whether and when to approach me. Gerry had told her about our encounter and how I had mentioned possibly leaving the Sherman facility. He had also told me about her and said she might be calling. I was open to it, feeling ready for the guidance for which I had been praying.

The Tuesday after Easter, I received a phone call from a number I didn't recognize and let my voicemail pick it up. A little while later, I listened to a message from Lauren. She introduced herself on the recording and asked me to get in touch with her if I needed anything—anything at all. She sounded so positive and encouraging, and I remember her ending with, "God bless. I'll be praying for you."

So I called her back.

"Hi, Lauren, this is Ramona Treviño, the woman Gerry told you about from Sherman?"

"Oh yes, hello, Ramona", she said. "I'm so glad you got my message. It's great to hear from you. Thanks so much for returning my call."

I immediately felt the light on the other end of the line, but I needed more information before I could let down my guard.

Lauren mentioned she was a friend of Gerry and worked for 40 Days for Life National, an organization that oversees campaigns to pray for an end to abortion. She said Gerry had shared with her at their closing event that I was looking to leave Planned Parenthood.

"I just wanted to see how I could help", Lauren said. "So, what has the Lord been doing in your life, Ramona? I'd love to hear what's been going on with you."

In a way, I was surprised by her question. Someone wanted to know what was going on with me? It was hard knowing what I should share, what would be most helpful, but I felt motivated to find the right words.

"Boy, well, let's see", I started. "I guess I've been realizing for a while now that I want a stronger relationship with God. When I started noticing the 40 Days for Life people outside my clinic, I was challenged in a good way, I think. I started searching my heart to look for ways I could make more of a positive impact, and one thing led to another."

I also told her I had been listening to Catholic radio, which had led me to reconsider contraception in my own life, and how that was now posing a conflict with my work at the clinic.

"Ramona," Lauren said after a while, "I just have to say, I'm really impressed by how you've been searching. It really sounds like you've been doing a lot of soul seeking, and I just want you to know that we'd like to help you make a change—if it feels right to you. But I also need to be honest and tell you it's going to be hard for us to do that while you're still at Planned Parenthood."

"Yes, I understand", I said, remembering Abby's story. "I know it would be better if I left sooner rather than later. But I've been a good manager, and I really think they'll understand. Plus, I was really hoping to get a few more paychecks under my belt, just to be safe."

Lauren gently reminded me of the difficulties Abby had experienced when she left Planned Parenthood. She also said that while she didn't want to scare me, she thought I should refrain from e-mailing anyone from work about my change of heart, and to reserve phone calls about it for after hours. "It's just better to play it safe."

"Yeah, you're probably right", I said. "I guess I'm just trying to figure out when the best time will be for my family."

Lauren said she completely understood, and I believed her. By this point, I had learned she was a Catholic, and that had given me comfort. I might not have opened up as readily without that. Besides, I had to trust. After all, I had asked God to lead me, and he couldn't really work in my life if I kept resisting the gifts he offered.

"Look, Ramona," Lauren said, "I just want you to know that there's a huge pro-life community in Dallas waiting to receive you lovingly, whenever you're ready. More than anything, I want you to know you're not alone. But I also realize it has to be your decision. So take some time, pray on it, and let me know what you think."

By the end of our conversation, my mind was going in several directions, but I was beginning to trust that no matter what I decided, I wouldn't be alone. I felt a peaceful reassurance of this when Lauren asked if we could pray together.

Afterward Lauren reminded me once more that whenever I was ready, she would be there for me; I wouldn't be jumping into nothing.

"Thanks, Lauren", I said. "That means a lot."

"Just one more thing," she added, "well, maybe two. First, Ramona, I want you to know, again, how impressed I am by your trust. I really mean that."

"Well, it's all I have now", I said, feeling my own words.

"It's true, and you can count on it, I promise", she said. "Second, I'm wondering if you'd be open to talking to someone else on our team, like Shawn Carney, the guy who helped Abby leave. He's been here before, after all."

"Sure, I'd be willing to talk to him."

"Okay, great. I'll work on setting up a call with the three of us. I'll let you know when Shawn's available, and we'll go from there. In the meantime, let's keep in touch."

Lauren and I did stay in contact through several more phone conversations over the next couple of days. Then on Friday, just after pulling into my driveway after work, we had a three-way phone call in which I was introduced to Shawn Carney.

First, we exchanged introductions. Then, after I offered a bit of my story, Shawn shared some of his insights, mainly retelling his experience with Abby, including her inevitable leap of faith and what she had experienced during that time, from his perspective.

I clung to every word. Even though I had read Abby's book, it seemed surreal that I was talking to the very person who had helped her get to the other side safely. I sensed he and Lauren were sincere in wanting to help me too.

When he was finished, both of them offered gentle encouragement, but they also reminded me, with a more urgent tone, of my culpability in the event I would stay at Sherman.

I was in tears, realizing the immensity of what was happening. It was as if my old life was beginning to crumble, the bricks tumbling fast now. I was seeing everything anew through the eyes of these people whom I felt certain God had placed on my path. But even as the earth seemed to wobble below, I felt immense relief in knowing of the reinforcements at my side.

"Ramona, I'm sure this is pretty heavy for you," Lauren said, seemingly sensing my thoughts, "but I feel called right now to share something that might help in this next step. This Sunday is Divine Mercy Sunday, and I really think Jesus wants to share with you that it's okay to simply trust in him. I'd encourage you to meditate on that at Mass this week and let it sink into your soul. God will protect you."

I didn't understand exactly what she meant, but her words assured me somehow. At the beginning of the conversation, I had been somewhat reserved. After all, I was dancing with what used to be the enemy just a few weeks ago. And yet both Lauren and Shawn were so patient with me that I couldn't help but feel I was moving toward rather than away from safety.

"I do want to leave", I said. "That's no longer a question in my mind. I'm just nervous about money. I really don't know how we're going to make it without something else lined up."

"We know it's scary," Lauren said, "but we're here for you. And trust us when we say leaving Planned Parenthood will bring peace to your life, just like Abby has experienced."

My feet were now on the edge of the cliff. I couldn't see the large hands ready to catch me, cradle me, and lift me back up, but I was willing to close my eyes and to believe in the possibility of again living a life of truth.

* * * * *

After that introductory call with Shawn and Lauren and my subsequent Divine Mercy Sunday experience, I felt an urgency to leave Planned Parenthood. I knew I needed to cast aside fear and not to let my attachment to money and other provisions stop me from doing what was right.

Through the words of that song at Mass, God seemed to be saying that he was going to use me in ways I couldn't yet see and that I needed to leave everything behind on "the seashore", trusting that I wouldn't be led astray.

That Monday, I woke with a sense of something weighing on my heart and the feeling that I needed to make a decision. What I had experienced at Mass the day before hadn't been a fleeting thing that could be ignored.

As I prayed through the morning at home about what to do, I began to hear an answer.

You need to have faith. The end of the month isn't going to cut it. You need to leave sooner.

Wanting to share this revelation, I picked up the phone to tell Lauren. It was almost as if I needed accountability.

"Well, I've made a decision, Lauren. I'm going to leave at the end of the month."

"That's wonderful, Ramona," she responded, "but I also want you to know that if the Lord calls you sooner, he'll be ready to catch you then just as well. Either way, you can definitely count on my prayers."

The next day I called her again. "Lauren, guess what?" I said. "I'm going to leave sooner, on Friday. You've convinced me. I need to trust." Lauren was right, after all. If I could trust God at the end of the month, I could trust him on Friday too. Either way, I knew I couldn't wait until summer.

Lauren shared her excitement with me and said she would be praying that I wouldn't be put in any more morally compromising situations, such as referring clients for abortions and distributing Plan B disbursement, in my final week on the job. She and Shawn also offered to review my letter of resignation.

The next day, Shawn, Lauren, and I set up another three-way conversation, this time to plan my exit from Planned Parenthood. Shawn advised that I immediately cut all ties to the company, omitting the standard two-week notice. We would discuss this idea and other details of the plan, he said, with Tom Brejcha of the Thomas More Society, which had offered free legal counsel to 40 Days for Life and had extended the same to me.

Lauren proposed that she and I meet face-to-face the following Monday and said she would like to introduce me to some of her pro-life contacts in Dallas as well as circulate my résumé.

Things were moving quickly.

* * * * *

Lauren and I met for the first time in person the following Monday. We agreed to make our meeting place Saint Michael's in McKinney because it was roughly halfway between the two of us.

I arrived first, and shortly thereafter, Lauren pulled up next to me. When we emerged from our vehicles, she immediately extended her arms for a hug.

"Well, I must say," she said, smiling, "Shawn was right. He told me he imagined that you looked like the Virgin of Guadalupe."

I blushed, giggling at the thought of it, and said, "Well, you're supposed to be dark-haired with glasses. I mean, you're a lawyer after all. I definitely wasn't expecting a blonde with green eyes. So much for stereotypes, I guess, right?"

"Oh, that's hilarious!" Lauren said.

I think we both felt the lightness of the icebreaker and the visuals that had gone with it.

"Excuse me for a moment", Lauren said. She returned to her car and pulled out a bouquet of roses and a framed picture. It was a rendition of Jesus with rays of red and white emanating from his heart. Below him was an inscription, "Jesus, I Trust in You."

"This is Divine Mercy", she said brightly. "Since you made the decision to leave the clinic on Divine Mercy Sunday, I feel like it's your feast day now."

"Thank you", I said, touched by the gesture, yet only vaguely remembering her having mentioned Divine Mercy Sunday earlier and certainly not fully grasping what it all meant.

She reached into her car again and this time retrieved a small stack of books. "I hope I'm not overwhelming you," Lauren said, "but I don't want to forget these." She explained that she had gone through her books the night before, looking for titles that had helped her come back to the faith after leaving it for a time in high school.

Among them were Alan Schreck's *Catholic and Christian*, Scott and Kimberly Hahn's *Rome Sweet Home*, and Christopher West's *Good News about Sex and Marriage*.

"Wow," I said, "thanks." I did feel a little overwhelmed but in an excited way. I couldn't wait to delve into the treasures Lauren was sharing with me. I was hungry to learn more.

Tucked in with the picture of Divine Mercy was a little card about Saint Faustina's vision and the Divine Mercy devotion. It explained how Jesus had promised extra grace on Divine Mercy Sunday, especially to the souls who had gone to confession and received Communion.

After listening numerous times to the Divine Mercy Chaplet on Catholic radio, I would later feel even more connected to the message. I would come to see Saint Faustina's vision of Divine Mercy as a precious offering to those trapped in sin—an unconditional invitation from Jesus to be reunited with him. The image of him with an overflowing heart and a kind, welcoming face says, "I offer you my forgiveness and mercy. I want to free you from the bondage of sin through love."

In hindsight, it seems to me nothing short of a miracle that God reached out to me in a profound way on Divine Mercy Sunday 2011—the very day Pope John Paul II, who had coined the term *culture of death*, was beatified. It is astonishing to me that the song "Lord When You Came to the Seashore" was one of his favorite hymns, "Barca" in Polish.

When I was working for Planned Parenthood, I was denying myself the close connection with God that I had experienced as a child. I would feel the stirring whenever I attended Mass, but with it came guilt, so I would stop going for a time, allowing myself to settle back into sin or complacency.

On that unforgettable Divine Mercy Sunday, God prompted my healing tears by offering his abundant grace. Jesus had already forgiven me in the sacrament of reconciliation, but on that Divine Mercy Sunday I was able to receive what I needed to forgive myself.

God's mercy is endless—more vast than all the grains of sand on all the beaches throughout the world. Because of his infinite mercy, there isn't any sin we can commit that he can't forgive.

I still experience feelings of unworthiness from time to time. But whenever the temptation to wallow in those feelings returns, I go back to the Divine Mercy picture on my mantle and read the words: "Jesus, I Trust in You." Each time, I see Jesus' hand reaching out and hear him saying, "Do you trust in me?"

"Yes, Jesus," I whisper, "I know you've got my back. I do trust in you."

14

Over the Rainbow

Like Dorothy in *The Wizard of Oz*, caught in the center of the twister, for several years I had been tossed about in the midst of the storm, trying to figure out what was up and what was down, searching for signs of life through the chaos of a cultural and personal tornado.

Then the little house of my soul had landed with a thud. The worst of the storm was over, but what might I find outside? Filled with a little anxiety and a whole lot of wonder, I planted my feet on the floor and began to walk toward the bright, colorful waiting world.

* * * * *

The Tuesday before I quit Planned Parenthood, I was eager to tie up loose ends and to leave things in the best shape possible. How would I want the next person to find the office? I wanted to prove to myself, if to no one else, that no matter where I worked, I would always leave behind a mark of integrity, unlike the way I had left WIC, with so much unraveled.

Any lingering worry about how things might go down disappeared when Linda reminded me that our nurse practitioner was helping at another clinic that was shorthanded, and because of this, we had cleared the schedule. It would be a no-client day, and we were free to do administrative work.

It seemed to be an answer to a prayer, leaving me a chance to breathe and to stay focused. After all, I had only a couple of days to pull everything together. And by then, my tolerance for deceit of any kind, including my own, was for good reason at a minimum. A day without clients would mean fewer chances to feel conflicted. As I set about my work, I couldn't help but hum a tune I had heard on the drive in.

"Boy, you sure seem like you're in a good mood, Ramona. It was a good weekend, I take it?" Linda asked.

"Well, yeah," I said, "I guess I am, and it was.... Linda, since it's just the two of us today, I have to tell you something, for your ears only."

"Sure. What is it, Ramona?"

"I'm resigning. Friday will be my last day."

"Wait a minute. You're joking, right?" she asked. Then, studying my face, she quickly added, "You're not joking, are you?"

"I'm sorry, Linda. I feel bad about leaving you. You know I'd love for you to come with me. But I've made up my mind. I've really gone through some huge realizations in the last week, and I just can't do it anymore."

"Oh, you know," she said, "I knew it was coming. But I just didn't know it would be this soon. And I have to admit, I'm going to miss you—a lot. I mean, I can't imagine being here without you."

She grabbed a nearby tissue and dabbed at her eyes.

"You know we'll keep in touch, right? I mean, it's not like our friendship hinges on us working here."

I had every confidence that Linda would be fine. She was a strong woman.

"Oh, I know," she said, "and don't you worry, Ramona. Nobody's going to get anything out of me."

"Hey, thanks", I said, giving her a hug. "I appreciate that more than you can know. Well, I've got a lot to do, so if you'd take care of the phones, I'm going to start clearing things out. Let's grab lunch later, okay?"

"Sounds good, and yes, you go ahead. I'll handle things here."

I spent the rest of the day going through our inventory and ordering enough supplies to ensure that the clinic could operate for the next couple of months.

Everything seemed to be progressing fairly uneventfully, much to my relief. But the next day, a client came in asking for a pregnancy test. While she waited in the lobby, I noticed her nervously flipping through some pamphlets.

The pregnancy test came back positive, and I delivered the news in one of the exam rooms in the back. After receiving confirmation of what she had feared, she put her head in her hands and began weeping.

"I can't do this. I have a little girl who's only three, and my boyfriend, he's never there for us. I think he's maybe even seeing someone else. I just can't—"

Dear Lord, help me to help her. There's nothing holding me back anymore; I can talk freely. By your grace, Lord, give me the courage to say what you would want me to say.

"Look," I said, putting a hand on her shoulder, "I know what you're going through. I've been there myself. I was pregnant as a teenager and lived with an abusive husband. I understand the fears you're experiencing. But I want you to know, above all else, that you do not have to make a decision you can't reverse, just because the father of your children isn't man enough to take care of you. There are good men out there—like my husband now. And there's someone out there for you, too; someone who will bend over backward to protect you and your kids. You can do this."

After taking in every word, she looked at me, and a slight smile formed on her face. Wiping away her tears, she said, "I came here feeling like that was the only answer, but I really didn't want to—"

"And you don't have to", I said. "Don't ever let anyone make you do anything out of fear. There are people who will walk you through this pregnancy and help you get to the other side of this. And when you're there, you'll meet this beautiful new person who will someday call you Mom."

As I told her about the local pregnancy help center, the heaviness I had seen on her face just a few minutes earlier vanished.

"Thank you so much", she said, putting her hand on her belly. "You're right. I am already a mom, and I would never be able to forgive myself if I'd had an abortion. Thank you!"

As I watched her leave, a lilt in her step, I smiled.

So this is what it's like to follow you all the way, Lord. Man, it feels great!

I felt then, as now, that the encounter wasn't a coincidence. Wanting me to have a taste of what was in store for my future, God gave me a glimpse of it in my final hours at Planned Parenthood through the gift of helping someone to discover the path of life.

* * * * *

The conference call with Tom Brejcha that Lauren had set up took place the Thursday before I left Planned Parenthood. Mostly we went over procedural things. Tom asked whether I had signed a contract, if I had any company property, things of that nature. He also reviewed my letter of resignation and made a few final comments.

I had kept the letter simple, as suggested, saying I was pursuing other opportunities that I would potentially miss out on by continuing in my current capacity and thanking my supervisors for allowing me the chance to be a manager. I stated that my resignation would take effect immediately.

I'll never forget what Tom said at the call's close, "Well, Ramona, slavery has been abolished, so you're free to leave." That's about what it felt like, and was I ever ready to taste freedom!

The next day, Friday, May 6, at 5:00 P.M., just after faxing the letter to the administrative offices of Planned Parenthood, I placed the original copy in an envelope on the front desk with the keys and walked out the door with Linda.

As we stood out front for a moment, she gave me a big hug. "I'm so going to miss you", she said. "Keep in touch, promise?"

"You got it."

I felt exhilarated on the drive home, as if a hundred-pound weight had just been lifted from my shoulders. "I can breathe!" I said out loud.

A heap of unknowns still lay ahead of me, especially concerning our finances, but I knew we would be okay for at least the next several months. My last paycheck would include a week of vacation pay and my remaining paid time off, plus my 401(k) funds.

We'll make it. I'm going to trust.

When I got home, the first thing I did was call Lauren. I just needed to share my relief with someone safe who would be as excited as I was. When I got her voicemail, I left a quick message, speaking my joy into the recorder.

Lauren told me later that she had been painting pottery with a friend when I called. With paint on her hands, she couldn't pick up the phone. "I remember running to go wash my hands, scurrying to the phone, and listening to your voicemail", she explained. "I just remember there was such excitement and peace in your voice."

After leaving the message for Lauren, I called Shawn. "Hey, Ramona, what's up?" he asked.

"I did it, Shawn. I'm done. I handed in my letter of resignation tonight."

"Ramona, that's great. I'm so happy for you", he said. "You're not going to regret this. It's going to get so much better from here. We're so proud of you."

That night, I slept soundly for the first time in many months.

* * * * *

When Lauren and I met in the Saint Michael's parking lot a few days later, there was no doubt that we both were feeling relief and in celebration mode. "Oh, I need to give you a big hug", she said immediately, extending her arms.

After showering me with the gifts I described earlier, Lauren shared her hopes for the rest of the day, most importantly her desire to introduce me to the Catholic Pro-Life Committee (CPLC) ladies of Dallas with whom she had arranged a visit. "They've all been praying for you and are so excited to meet you," she said, "and I wouldn't count out the possibility of them having some job leads, if not today, then hopefully another time soon."

The whole pro-life world was still so new to me that I felt as if I had just stepped onto a new planet. So many things looked the same, yet everything was different. My notion of the CPLC group, for instance, was pretty vague. The week before, after seeking my permission, Gerry had given Lauren the okay to share my résumé discreetly with the group in the event that an opening might come onto their radar. I had even talked to one of them, Aurora Tinajero, director of the group's Spanish ministries, by phone. But it definitely felt as if I were on some kind of mystery adventure.

"I'm up for anything", I said. Lauren seemed so optimistic that it was hard to say no. I felt I needed to trust her lead, even if I was a little nervous.

"Okay, great. So why don't I drive?" she said.

On the ride into Dallas, Lauren was giddy and chatty. It was hard not to be excited with her, hearing her bubble over with enthusiasm. She had a nice balance, however, with an equal ability to be very serious when the situation called for it.

"Do you see that gap there between those buildings?" Lauren asked as we closed in on the heart of the city. "That's where the Aaron's late-term abortion facility once stood. I used to sidewalk-counsel out in front of it, before law school."

Lauren then shared how Dallas had organized the second 40 Days for Life campaign in front of that facility during the winter of 2004. "Just a couple years later," she said, "that facility closed down forever."

"When and where was the first 40 Days for Life campaign?" I asked.

"That one happened in Bryan / College Station, Texas, a few months before, in the fall of 2004."

Adding more pieces to the puzzle, she told me how David Bereit, the director of a small pro-life activist organization called the Coalition for Life, along with Shawn and his wife, Marilisa, and a volunteer named Emily, had been praying for an answer to reduce abortion in their area. The answer God gave them turned into 40 Days for Life.

"It all came together in a matter of about a week," Lauren said, "but the effort activated a thousand people and prompted a 28 percent drop in abortions in that community alone. It wasn't much later that they got the call from the Dallas CPLC asking to jump on board."

Lauren explained that the first national campaign took place in the fall of 2007, with more than 89 cities participating. As of that past spring, 40 Days for Life had grown to 247 campaigns throughout the United States, Canada, and 7 other countries. "The results have been amazing", she said. "In every campaign, lives have been saved and hearts changed."

As she talked, I listened, mesmerized by this world that had existed right under my nose but had been invisible to me.

"Wow. I just can't believe I've been so blind", I said. "I feel like I've been living under a rock."

It was true. Until then I really had little idea of what had been going on behind the scenes of this public debate, which ironically was centered largely on the place from which I had just fled. Oh, there were signs of it, and I could have followed through when I saw the red flags waving. Instead, I had chosen to ignore them all.

"We're getting closer now", Lauren announced. "The CPLC office is just a couple blocks up."

Lauren had promised she would gently walk me through this introduction, and I trusted her, but it was still a little intimidating. My stomach started churning. Even with Lauren's summary of the women involved in the CPLC and their significance in the Dallas pro-life scene, I wondered how I would be perceived. Were they really excited to see me, a former Planned Parenthood manager? Now that I saw this world more from their vantage point, a part of me wondered.

When we walked into the CPLC office, signs of a Catholic presence were everywhere. I found it refreshing to look around and see holy pictures, a crucifix, and Scripture verses, and I was especially drawn to a statue of Mary holding Jesus as a baby. It was like walking into a house owned and decorated by a long-lost relative.

Soon I felt I was among friends. Becky Visosky, communications director, greeted me warmly with a smile and a handshake. And when I heard Aurora's voice, I recognized it right away from our earlier phone conversation.

"Ramona, it's so nice to finally meet you," she said, "and look how beautiful you are." She was definitely more sweet aunt than intimidating stranger.

Karen Garnett, the executive director, also popped out to greet me, as did Ellen Rossini from development.

After a while, Lauren led me into a small conference room. Motioning me to the head of a large table, she said, "Why don't you sit right here, Ramona."

In a way, I felt as if I had just entered an FBI interrogation room. I was in the hot seat, and one by one, in filed the others—experts who wanted to talk to me. Most of them seemed friendly, but I had a hard time reading one of them: Patty Sherrod, director of ministries. Though Patty had seemed friendly in our introduction, I sensed more reservation from her.

"So, Ramona, you're Catholic?" Patty asked after a while.

"Yes, I am", I said, pretty sure I knew what she was thinking. She was wondering how any Catholic could have joined forces with a company like Planned Parenthood. It did seem incongruous from the outside, but I wanted a chance to explain.

Lord, you know who I am, and you know I don't need to defend myself here. Help me to be authentic to these women. Help me to be myself so they'll see me as you do.

After Karen led a group prayer that ended with a Hail Mary, I relaxed.

This isn't a job interview, Ramona. Just speak from your heart.

"Well, thanks for that prayer," I began, "and it's really nice to meet all of you. I'm sure it must seem strange that a Catholic girl could ever work for Planned Parenthood. Unfortunately, I'm not the only one. Let me try to explain how it happened with me."

As I shared some of the key factors that had led me into the company and what I had discovered since, I watched the transformation in Patty's body language. By the time I had finished sharing, I could tell I had passed her test.

The more we all talked, the more comfortable I became. Any barriers I had perceived at the start faded, so much so that at one point, I just blurted out what was on my mind.

"What I'd really love to see happen," I said, "is for Planned Parenthood to shut down forever."

At that point, the whole room erupted into happy laughter.

Even Patty was visibly more relaxed. In fact, she was laughing the hardest, it seemed. "Wait a second," she said, still smiling and jokingly grabbing a pen, "I've got to write that down!"

"Ramona, we're so happy to hear you say that," Karen said, "because we've been praying for the same thing. And we're getting closer. We also want you to know how proud of you we are. Your actions make such a powerful statement. You are doing God's work now, and he is so pleased."

Later Lauren shared that while everyone in the room had been cautiously optimistic that my exit had been genuine, by this point in the meeting, I had convinced them that my feelings and transformation were true.

"Well, we're definitely behind you," Karen said, "and if we hear of a job opening that would be appropriate, we'll let you or Lauren know right away."

Later, Karen told me how refreshing it had been to hear me talk not only about abortion but also about contraception and its dangers—a layer many overlook.

By the end of the meeting, everyone was hugging me, welcoming me into the fold. Any sense of being alone was now history.

"Ramona, this is just the beginning", Lauren said as we walked back to her car. "There's a whole world here that's been in motion for a while now, committees and organizations that exist solely to support women, children, and families, and to guide the culture back around to love. I can't wait to see what God has in store for you."

On the way home, I tried to absorb it all, but it was a lot to take in. After all, I had just been introduced to a dimension of my Church, and the world, that I had never known existed. All my life, I had sensed that the Catholic Church was a place of refuge, yet it was more a concept than a lived reality. But I had just been shown the hands and feet of Christ saving lives and souls.

Indeed, I had stepped from a world of gray tones into one of vibrantly colorful scenes and was left uttering, "Lord, I have a feeling I'm not at Planned Parenthood anymore." I had just noticed the ruby slippers on my feet and soon would meet other comrades—the Scarecrow, the Tin Man, the Cowardly Lion, and others. Lauren, like the beautiful, sparkly Glinda the Good Witch, was nearby, smiling me into this new world with her star-topped wand. And off in the distance, a yellow brick road beckoned.

But there would be moments when I would hesitate to go forward, like Dorothy, hung up on practical matters. This colorful world intrigued me, but it was important to stay grounded, to secure a job, and to find my way home.

There were also the usual dangers inherent in any new adventure. In the coming months, I would meet up many times with an ugly green witch—my spiritual foe who threatened me at every turn. But whenever she would appear, Glinda and the others would nudge me through with encouragement, assuring me that I had already found home, right in my own backyard.

15

The Closing

Linda and I continued to stay in touch, just as we had promised, and in June she called with some interesting news.

"Ramona, the vice president came into the Sherman clinic yesterday. Guess what?"

"The Sherman clinic's closing?" I said, half-kidding.

"Yes. It'll be shut down by August."

Though surprising, the news didn't come as a complete shock. Over the past couple of years, corporate had made it clear that it was running scared over its bottom line. Since Sherman had been doing better than some of the larger facilities, however, I hadn't guessed it would be among the immediate casualties.

But good managers didn't come easily, either, and though I didn't feel wholly responsible for the imminent closing, I wondered if my leaving had been the proverbial straw that broke the camel's back for the Sherman location.

"What are you gonna do, Linda?" I asked.

"Well," she said, "I'm hoping I can move to another site. I mean, I don't have any other options in my mind right now. I guess time will tell."

In the end, Planned Parenthood denied her request for a site transfer, citing as the reason the fact that she had once been written up. When Linda learned of the severance package they were offering her, she called me in tears.

"Can you believe this, Ramona? After all the time and energy I've given them?"

The company's decision seemed unfair to me, and I wondered whether Planned Parenthood had questioned Linda's allegiance. Perhaps because of our friendship, they had decided not to risk another breach.

Whatever the case, God blessed Linda during that difficult time. The client schedules had been cleared from July until the August closing, leaving her the opportunity to work her final months client-free and to focus on studying and searching for another job.

I thanked God for freeing my friend from Planned Parenthood, and I was convinced she would be all right.

* * * * *

I didn't feel the full impact of the Sherman clinic's impending closure right away. Since so much of my journey had been internal, it took me a while to grasp the wider implications of its shutdown, particularly how the pro-life community would perceive the news.

Apparently, I had been helping the pro-life cause for months before I walked away, or so I learned at the closing celebration organized by the 40 Days for Life team.

Among the prominent local pro-lifers I met that day was Melva Kittrell. As director of the area's Pregnancy Care Center, she had been, in Planned Parenthood's eyes, one of the enemies. But I had seen her facility as a resource for the women who came in with needs we couldn't adequately address.

As Melva and I chatted, I could see the wheels turning in her mind. At last she said, "So now I know who was sending all those women over to our clinic. We couldn't figure out what was going on. In all the years I've been with the Pregnancy Care Center, we'd never seen referrals from a Planned Parenthood facility."

"I did refer women over there, yes," I said, "and more and more often in these last months."

"Well, God bless you. What an honor to meet you. You are a courageous young woman."

As I shook Melva's hand, my mind flashed back to an administrator visit at our clinic the previous year.

The administrator, who had been going through materials in preparation for an audit, summoned me with, "Uh, Ramona, can you come here for a second?"

Holding a card from our Rolodex with the Pregnancy Care Center's handwritten name and number on it, she said, "We need to get rid of this. We don't really refer people here."

"Okay," I said, "but do you mind if I ask why?"

"Well," she said, "this place isn't exactly what we'd call pro–Planned Parenthood. Have you referred people there?"

"Yes, if it seemed necessary."

"Okay, well, you'll need to stop."

When I worked for Planned Parenthood, our clinic charged twenty-five dollars for a simple pregnancy test, whereas the Pregnancy Care Center offered it for free. For many low-income women, the difference was crucial. Because it seemed only right to refer them to a place that could save them some money, I did not understand my administrator's reaction.

I was still naive about the existence of the pro-life / pro-choice battle that had been shooting off rounds for years. I knew that some people believed abortions were okay and others didn't, but I hadn't been paying attention to the war cries of each side.

The day of the administrator visit, however, I heard canons firing and realized it was probably time to be more attentive to them.

* * * * *

As the day of the closing drew near, I more fully recognized the Holy Spirit at work.

After telling me about the pro-life community's plans to commemorate the event, Lauren said, "Ramona, we'd really like you to speak at the closing celebration."

"Well, I don't know. I mean, I feel like this was more God's doing than anything. What would I even say?"

"Well, it's true that the Holy Spirit set this in motion," Lauren said, "but you were a big part of it, Ramona. In a way, you're a physical representation of what's been happening spiritually. I mean, you don't have to speak if you'd like to wait, but it might be really special for you to say a few words to thank all the prayer volunteers who were out there."

I remembered then how Lauren had shared Gerry's reaction to my leaving Planned Parenthood. He had responded matter-of-factly, almost as if taking it for granted that God and prayer would prompt that kind of change. And Linda had mentioned how one of the nurse practitioners had commented, "I don't understand why they're closing Sherman and not McKinney, since Sherman sees twice as many clients."

Evidence of the divine hand couldn't be ignored. What if God were blessing those who had been praying through my decision to leave? If so, didn't I owe them a few words so that the blessing could be properly honored?

"Okay," I said, "I guess I can do that." But I wondered, with butterflies in my stomach, where all this could possibly be going.

* * * * *

About a week before the closing celebration, our doorbell rang. The FedEx truck was parked in front of our house, but I had no idea why, since I hadn't been expecting anything. Maybe Eugene had ordered something and forgotten to tell me.

After signing for the envelope bearing an "overnight delivery" label, I noticed the return address from Planned Parenthood. While the driver headed back to the truck, I stood at the entryway and ripped open the package.

It was a letter from corporate reminding me that I had signed some paperwork committing to confidentiality, and though I had a right to my opinion, I needed to honor my commitment to keep details of my work at Planned Parenthood to myself.

Just that week, an article had come out on LifeSiteNews.com about my decision to leave. Perhaps that had prompted the letter, I thought. Either way, there was no doubt in my mind that the tone and words were meant to intimidate.

"Okay, here we go", I said, chuckling while closing the door behind me. "If this is the way you want it, then let's go."

I knew from Abby's story what Planned Parenthood did when her departure from the company went public, but having talked to the Thomas More lawyer, I felt protected and assured.

That night, however, the voices of doubt crept in. "Are you sure you're ready for this, Ramona? Was it worth it?" they sneered. I would need to do more to reinforce my spiritual armor, apparently.

Just remember, Mona, you have people behind you, and you did the right thing.

As I sat down to write up some notes for the closing event, I said, "Okay, God, I hope you're still with me because I think I'm really going to need you now. This is my chance to help you shine. I don't want to blow it."

* * * * *

I felt God's response, especially through others he sent to help me, such as Becky from the CPLC.

As communications director, Becky became a crucial part of my transition into this new world. Because the CPLC had asked me to be their keynote speaker at the upcoming fall kickoff event for the 40 Days for Life–Dallas campaign, an event they sponsored annually, they naturally became the ones to write the press release announcing my departure from Planned Parenthood and the fact that I would keynote their event.

Once the press release went out, Becky also became my official media contact—because of my connection to their event and because of her graciously volunteering to help. The CPLC also sponsored a pro-life Boot Camp for teens every summer, and that became my very first speaking engagement shortly after leaving Planned Parenthood.

Both Becky and Lauren worked to ensure that I would be protected as I worked my way into this new world, conferencing with me quite often about personal safeguards as my story was brought into the public eye. For example, I agreed that, initially, I would do interviews only with friendly religious media.

Becky also helped to prepare me for how the pro-life side would handle the closing of my former workplace. Both she and Lauren wanted to ensure that Linda and I would be protected; thus, the CPLC waited to send the press release until after the facility closed and Linda had left Planned Parenthood. She also clued me in on how many Planned Parenthood administrators receive e-mails from the CPLC to keep tabs on their work.

With Becky's help, we scheduled the press release alerting the media of the closing celebration for August 24, the day after Sherman's closing. The release was picked up by pro-life news outlets fairly quickly, resulting in articles in both LifeNews and LifeSiteNews, which included an interview with me. When I pulled up the article online and saw myself staring back, it hit me. *Well, Mona, there's no turning back now. You're in it for the long haul. This is it.*

Though I wouldn't have chosen the spotlight at that time, when I still felt a little shaky over my new direction, I knew the publicity would help me to claim my new path and possibly educate others.

No one ever said sacrifice wouldn't be involved. After all, I know of another who did plenty of that before leaving this world, and if he could endure it, surely he could help me to endure whatever sacrifice I might have to make.

* * * * *

On the morning of August 28, the day of the closing celebration, sweat beads kept dripping down my temples. We were in the dog days of summer, and I was three months pregnant with child number three.

At least some of those drops may have been from nerves. Stepping out of the car with Eugene and Lorena at the former Sherman facility, I spotted David Bereit, national director of 40 Days for Life.

This would be my first in-person meeting with David, and I was more than a little nervous. "Oh, Lord, here we go", I mumbled. "God, please be with me."

In all, about fifty people had gathered for the event, including members of the 40 Days for Life–Sherman leadership, the CPLC, several workers from the Pregnancy Care Center, and a group of people from the community. I noticed a reporter with a notepad and pen, and later found out that she was from the *Dallas Observer*. Several people had cameras, and since the facility is located on a public right-of-way, we were fairly exposed to passersby.

David was over by the tent that had been set up in front of the facility for shelter, and media interviews, if needed. Gerry was setting up a microphone for the speakers. Despite the heat, the atmosphere was definitely celebratory, with lots of smiling.

As I walked toward the crowd, Lauren waved me over to the tent. "Hey, Ramona," she called, "come on over and meet David!"

After talking a bit, David casually mentioned that the event would be videotaped. Realizing this wasn't going to be a small, private affair, I tried not to panic and simply smiled and said, "Okay."

Suddenly, my concerns seemed less about finances and job security and more about what Planned Parenthood and others might say about me. Was I really ready for this?

Several hundred yards away stood my old clinic. I had shared some laughs with Linda in there, helped a few women smile, and experienced a million regrets. Now the building seemed to be glaring at me.

I was the one out on the sidewalk now, and the clinic where I had spent the last three years of my life was vacant. A year ago, I couldn't have guessed I would be standing in this spot, in this way.

As I chatted more with David and the others, I began to feel less on the outside. This felt more right than the world I had just left. Everyone was so nice and seemed so genuinely grateful for my taking part in this special day.

And I liked the feeling of doing something edifying, for once.

Lord, if this is what you're going to be calling me to, allow me to do it well and to remember always to give you the glory. Jesus, I trust in you.

After Lauren and Gerry introduced me and handed me the microphone, I looked out at the faces, some familiar and others new, and noticed that all eyes were on me.

"I want to start off by saying thank you," I began, "first of all, to God, and to give all the glory to God, because without him none of this is possible." I thanked my family, too, for having come out in the insufferable heat.

"Prayer is the most powerful connection that we have with God," I continued, "and that's why we're celebrating today—the power of prayer and the power of the prayers of all of you standing here today.

"As most of you know by now, I was the manager of this Planned Parenthood facility for three years, and during the spring of this year, you could say, everything changed."

* * * * *

Though I knew about the closing before it went public, I had kept it under wraps for Linda's sake. By mid-August, anyone who showed up at the clinic would have seen a note on the locked door announcing its official closing date, but still only a limited number of people knew about it.

After the closing celebration, however, David uploaded the video, and by the next morning it had gone live. Seemingly overnight it had received fifteen thousand hits. An online article about the closing celebration referred to me as "the next Abby Johnson". I certainly didn't feel that, but obviously something bigger than little Ramona was at work.

That morning Linda was at her new station at the Gainesville clinic, where she would finish her time with Planned Parenthood. Our area supervisor, Julie, had joined Linda to help her with boxing up files and tending to other matters that needed attention prior to her leaving.

According to Linda, while they were in the middle of all the commotion, Julie yelled out suddenly, "Oh my God, I can't believe this. Ramona was at the pro-life rally in front of the Sherman clinic yesterday!"

A link to the YouTube video of the closing celebration had just been sent to Julie, and she was viewing it on her phone.

"Hey, can you send that to my e-mail?" Linda asked, walking into her office to view it privately.

By then, others had crowded around Julie. As Linda watched it from her computer, she heard Julie saying, "Why is she doing this? I always thought she was such a dedicated manager. I don't get it."

Later that day, Julie questioned Linda, asking her how long I had been feeling dissatisfied with Planned Parenthood. They were speculating that I had learned they were going to close the Sherman facility and had left for that reason.

"No," Linda said, "I don't think she had a clue we were closing. At least she didn't say anything to me. Besides, she can do anything she wants now. She doesn't work here anymore. And I don't see anything wrong with it. I'm pro-life, too."

16

The Fruits of Trust

Standing at the entrance of the small auditorium at the University of Dallas–Irving a month earlier, I made a quick Sign of the Cross with sweaty palms. "This is it", I said, following Lauren and Gerry to the center of the room.

Looking out into the crowd, I took in the faces of the pro-life youth with all their smiles and fervor and felt in awe all over again to realize this world had existed without my knowing it.

The pro-life Boot Camp for high school students was an annual event sponsored by the CPLC to ignite youth about the problem of abortion and other related attacks against human life and to propose concrete ways to stand up to them.

Each night ended with a speaker, and I had been invited to join Lauren and Gerry on the night of their talk. We decided not to promote my arrival beforehand, however. It would be a surprise. The closing of the Sherman clinic still hadn't taken place, and we remained cautious about timing.

Following Lauren's and Gerry's introductions, the students welcomed me with resounding applause. The vibrant, young crowd put me at ease immediately and helped me to look forward to what would come next.

In many ways, it seems natural that young people would be the ones to woo me into this new phase of my life. Children had always helped to ground me, keeping me near to both God and my own inner child. I also sensed they would offer a kinder, gentler reception than the adult world could.

And they did. After I talked about my personal story for about twenty minutes, the kids all stood up and began clapping wildly. It took me a few moments to realize I was getting a standing ovation. I was overwhelmed, and tears of happiness began forming in my eyes.

"You did great, Ramona. I just knew they'd love you", Lauren said. "Boy, you really seem to have a knack for speaking."

Sharing my experience had been so much easier than I had imagined. Around young people there were no pretenses. No one judged; they simply listened, even hung on to my every word. It seemed I might have something of value to share with them.

As the clapping continued, I felt my heart expanding, my soul lifting. The freedom to call things what they are and not to feel inhibited by an overbearing force promoting untruths, felt liberating beyond words.

I didn't know where God would take me exactly, but I knew that a life of giving felt altogether different from what I had been doing for most of my adulthood. I was ready to embrace that for good.

* * * * *

Prior to Boot Camp, the thought of working in the pro-life movement had never occurred to me. I had a teenager and a preschooler at home— mouths to feed and their futures to consider. Our income had just been sliced in half. I needed a job and almost anything would do, so long as it was pleasing to God.

And so the search began.

My days became filled with job hunting online and perusing classifieds, in between tending to Elijah. I knew it might take a while to find the right fit, but in the background, the clock ticked. Our bit of financial padding wouldn't last indefinitely.

While I sifted through the options, Lauren stayed in touch, sharing more and more of the world I had missed while I tried to find my place in another.

In fact, what had begun as a relationship born out of the need to survive was developing into a real friendship. For several months now, Lauren and I had been chatting by phone two or three times a week, and eventually the frequency of our contact increased. The spiritual bond alone—something I hadn't really experienced before to this degree— made it possible for us to feel as if we had known one another for longer than a couple of months.

In that time, I had come to realize that I hadn't been the only one stepping out in faith. Lauren, too, had been leaning harder than ever on God. After all, by encouraging me to take risks, she was doing the same.

I still had a lot to process, and Lauren had become my go-to person. I felt safe confiding in her.

I don't know how I could have done it without her. At times, I was a wreck as I tried to discern God's will for my life. I had messed up so many times that I was terrified of making another move that could turn out wrong.

One night, feeling particularly emotional, I shared my deepest fears with Lauren, through tears.

"I don't know, Lauren. I just can't figure out what it is I'm supposed to be doing now", I said. "Maybe God just wants me to suffer for a while for what I did at Planned Parenthood."

At that point, Lauren got very quiet, which scared me at first because I took it as a confirmation that I had just said something true, that God was punishing me.

But then she said, "Oh no, Ramona. On the contrary, I think the Lord has been waiting all this time to bless you. Our God is a God of mercy. He's been waiting to shower you with blessings!"

Her words were not what I was expecting, but they were words I needed to hear. It was as if God himself had said them. It really didn't make sense, if God had led me this far, for him to stand back now to watch me flounder and fail. How could I serve him curled up in a fetal position?

Lauren had shared with me that each time she had heard me speak, she sensed a real gift in me in—something out of the ordinary. But she followed her thoughts about my future with, "Above all else, you need to do whatever the Holy Spirit is calling you to."

It was refreshing not to feel pressure one way or the other, just gentle encouragement. The problem was that it meant I would need to figure out on my own where the Holy Spirit was leading. That was both freeing and terrifying.

"O Lord, what are you calling me to?" I would whisper over and over again, wishing for a crystal ball.

As I went about mothering and taking care of our home, my mind would wander back to what I had just been through and forward to what could lie ahead. So many insights came to me as I took in the past and considered the future.

I was experiencing a paradigm shift in the way I looked at the world. When Barbara McGuigan reached into my heart that day in the driveway, I couldn't escape the reality that for years I had been washing my hands clean for the sake of what I thought was peace, but in doing so, I had been denying myself a life in God's grace.

Ramona, one day you're going to die, and you're going to be standing before God. And he'll ask, "Did you know babies were being ripped apart limb by limb?" Words won't be enough then. You'll have to make an account for your actions.

A job promising convenience, an impressive-sounding title, and recognition of my work ethic hadn't been enough. None of that had brought the inner peace for which I yearned.

I started remembering details, such as how college students used to call our office to survey the mindset of their fellow Texans on life issues. "So what do you think of Margaret Sanger?" one had asked. "Did you know she was a racist?"

"I don't know anything about that", I had answered weakly, knowing full well I could easily Google her name. But I didn't want to. Knowing that the moment I heard the truth, I would need to make a choice, I deliberately avoided looking too deeply at anything.

And then there was the Church and the way in which I had turned away from her when things got challenging. To live with the inner conflict of working for a company directly involved in activities that the Church teaches are wrong, while calling myself Catholic, I necessarily had to view some Church teachings as misfires. I couldn't accept contraception as a grave evil when my job required me to accept it as a solution.

Besides, Eugene and I had been using contraception ourselves. Elijah's premature birth had prompted Eugene and me to conclude he would be our last. My doctor had warned me that my endometriosis would likely prevent another pregnancy anyway, so we figured the deal was sealed.

In a way, I had been viewing the Church as a crabby parent enforcing a "no candy before dinner" rule. It wasn't such a big deal to sneak a bit of chocolate before supper every once in a while, was it? But I knew now that rather than existing to make her children miserable, the Church has rules in place so that they might live healthfully—dinner first, dessert afterward.

Ravenous to read literature about the Church's true teachings, I was grateful to come across a tape by Janet Smith about the dangers of artificial birth control called *Contraception, Why Not?* I also read *Humanae*

Vitae, the encyclical explaining the Church's vision for sexual intimacy. In these I found a beautiful presentation of love that seemed worth pursuing.

Even before I left Planned Parenthood, Eugene and I had begun learning Natural Family Planning (NFP). There are a few different methods of NFP, but all of them help a woman to know when she is fertile. With this knowledge a couple can avoid pregnancy by limiting sexual intimacy to infertile times or achieve pregnancy by having sexual intimacy during fertile times.

NFP allowed Eugene and me to avoid pregnancy without using contraception. Chemical-free, our sexual intimacy produced an unanticipated "side effect". Rather than being intimate less, we found ourselves in the marital embrace more often than ever. There were times during my years on the pill when I had felt like an object at my husband's disposal, no matter how pure his urges may have been. But now I felt honored and cherished.

Around Elijah's fourth birthday, a yearning I had felt to have another child seemed stronger than ever. I had shared my desire with Eugene, but our fears and even a little selfishness played a role in our postponing pregnancy, along with our doubts that conception would even be possible.

One evening, just a month after leaving Planned Parenthood, I noticed on my NFP chart that I had entered my fertile phase. The children were asleep, and Eugene and I were finally able to share some time alone in our bedroom. As we embraced and shared a kiss, I chuckled and said to him, "You know I'm fertile right now, don't you?"

His kisses progressed and so did his caresses as he said, "It's okay."

I looked at him in shock and replied, "Are you sure? You know we can conceive right now, don't you?"

He nodded a sweet yes and said, "It's whatever God wants."

A couple of weeks later, the pregnancy test confirmed it: we were expecting. The timing of my third pregnancy would seem, from outside accounts, on the irrational side. After all, I had not yet settled into a new career. But I had promised God fidelity in all aspects of my life, and surrendering our wills to his had led us to new life.

Learning of my baby's existence was about the best news I had had in the past several months. After leaving Planned Parenthood, I had faced a rejection in my pursuit of a job for the first time ever.

"Jesus, I trust in you. I do", I would say, looking yet again at Jesus in the Divine Mercy image. "My life is in your hands."

* * * * *

When the phone rang, I jumped to answer.

"Can I speak with Ramona Treviño, please?" asked the unknown voice.

"Yes," I said, "you've reached her."

The call was from a life insurance company in need of an agent. A few days later I interviewed, made the final cut, and was offered the job. For the next several weeks, I attended classes to get my license, and despite feeling nervous, I did well on the test and passed with flying colors.

But three days into my new job, I began to feel unsettled. My work required selling Medicare to senior citizens, and I had a distressing sense I was once again exploiting people for company gain. I didn't want to be in another morally questionable position.

I called Lauren to talk with her privately on my cell phone one evening. In the quiet of our backyard, I let it all out.

"Lauren," I said, "I just don't think I can do this. What's wrong with me?"

"What do you feel like you should do?" she said. "It sounds like that may not be the right place for you."

A couple of weeks earlier, on break during the insurance training, I had gotten into a conversation with a Spanish-speaking custodian who, as it turned out, had been going through some difficulties in her home life. Even though I knew members of our group were conversing in the other room, I couldn't pull myself away from her. She needed advice, not only practical but spiritual, and I felt compelled to offer it.

When I indicated that it was time for me to rejoin my group, the woman smiled and said, "Gracias."

"No problema, Señora. Vaya con Dios."

That moment kept coming back to me, because it felt so natural to talk to her. It didn't escape me that maybe God was calling me to some kind of ministry work. But what kind exactly, and more importantly, would it help pay the bills? Money remained a constant worry.

During this time, Lauren called me, asking to meet in our usual spot so that she could give me something. What I didn't know was that a group of pro-life people from the Dallas area had pooled together some resources to help our family during that uncertain time.

In Saint Michael's parking lot a few days later, Lauren presented me with an envelope and her usual smile. When I opened it up, I found a card with signatures and a check for $1,250.

I began crying on the spot, out of gratitude and a little relief, too. This was more than words and kind sentiments. This was God's love and encouragement, shown through his people in their gift. I could almost hear him saying, "Hang in there. I have big plans for you. I will provide."

A few days later, I sent in another letter of resignation. Unlike last time, though, I didn't feel frightened. I knew God would lead me and keep our family safe.

* * * * *

It wasn't long before I landed another job in Sherman, just around the corner from my old clinic. I worked for a short-term loan agent, giving high-interest loans to people who were generally poor.

Soon, that also began to feel wrong.

My job required me to go into the area neighborhoods, often at night, to collect debts that hadn't been paid.

"I don't like this", Eugene finally said. "I'm not okay with you going out into these shady neighborhoods at night and trying to get money from people who probably don't have it to give. It's dangerous, Mona."

Eugene hadn't been comfortable with me at Planned Parenthood for safety reasons, and now he felt I was unsafe once again, especially given my condition. I couldn't blame him; he was just fulfilling his role as my protector.

Three months into that loan job, fifty dollars went missing from one of my money drawers. I had never made a mistake with money before, not ever in my time with Planned Parenthood or since. My manager, however, had been struggling with an addiction to pain killers. Half the time she was strung out, and I couldn't help but wonder if she had stolen the money.

I vented to Lauren yet again, and she said, "Ramona, look, I know this is a hard time for you, but I'm really seeing something else. I think God doesn't want you to get comfortable anywhere right now because he's got other plans for you."

As we talked, we started looking at the situation from other angles, including the possibility that God might be calling me to pray for my supervisor. Seeing it that way made it feel less about me and more about someone else, which felt good, even if I remained slightly uneasy.

Just a few weeks earlier, I had stood at the old Sherman clinic site, celebrating its closing with others and feeling something powerful moving within me. And a month earlier, students had given me a standing ovation after hearing my story. My words seemed to be stirring hearts.

Is this what you want for me, God? To share my story with others, with the hope that it will inspire them?

If so, how could I possibly have a nine-to-five job and be on a speaking circuit, while keeping up with the even more important duty of caring for my young family? I no longer desired a job just to have an income. I was beginning to feel, as Lauren had been hinting, that I had more to give—to my family and to God.

In the end, my baby put a stop to my job with the loan office. I had been vomiting frequently, and when I started having contractions in my first trimester, my doctor advised bed rest.

With that, I started progesterone injections to prevent preterm delivery, put in my notice once again, and stepped back to watch for the divine signs of what might be next.

* * * * *

Christmas 2011 was one of the most special times of my life, in part because we had nothing and so everything became a gift. Rather than being caught up in the number of presents we could accumulate, we prayed that God would provide our daily bread. And little by little, through the love of the new people in our lives, he came through.

First I received a gift card in the mail from an anonymous person. Then other envelopes arrived, most signed, all from the pro-life community. Opening one of these I said to Eugene, "I can't believe this— it's a hundred-dollar cash card for the grocery store." I was so relieved by the thought of being able to make a nice meal for our family at a time when the cupboards looked somewhat empty.

I'll admit that in the weeks leading up to Christmas, I was beginning to wonder if God had disappeared. But with that showering of love came a renewed sense of hope and faith and a more fervent trust in the true message of Christmas.

Flipping the calendar over to January 1, 2012, I sensed the worst was over and the best just beginning.

* * * * *

On March 5, we welcomed a new and precious little boy into our family and, not long after, asked Lauren and her husband, Peter, to serve as his godparents.

Our baby, Philip, has become the most palpable manifestation of the world we've claimed through faithfulness to Christ. More important even than a new career or circle of friends, a brand-new person, an eternal being who wouldn't have existed if I had still been working for Planned Parenthood, had joined the earth and our lives.

While nursing him, he would reach out his hand to touch my face, catching his fingers in my hair. After gently removing them, I would pull him closer, loving the feeling of him next to me.

As my husband held our beautiful boy with almond eyes, plump cheeks, and deep dimples, I would say, "Can you imagine, Eugene, if he weren't here?"

"Nah, Mona, not a chance", he would answer, throwing Philip into the air and catching him as the baby showered us with the sweetness of his giggles.

Looking back through my earlier pregnancies, starting with Lorena's, I realized there wasn't a time, ever, that God had failed me. But I had failed myself by allowing fear to rule my life. I know now that spiritual bondage leads to death, and if not physical death, then most certainly death of the soul.

It's so tempting to live our lives in fear, to let the messages of the world take us under, to convince us that what is wrong is right. But if we're to be free, we must learn to trust the one who is love. When we do, the fruits will appear everywhere.

17

Lorena's Song

May 2013

Sometimes we're called to be exceedingly patient as we await God's blessings. And then one fine day it becomes obvious that in the course of our lives God has been lavish with his love.

It wasn't until Lorena's senior year in high school that the abundance and depth of God's love fully penetrated my soul.

She had always been a delightful child, but there were times growing up when Lorena retreated a bit and turned very shy. Then in middle school, she tried out for a play and earned a role that nudged her out of her shell. She had fallen in love with acting.

During her freshman year, Lorena sat in on a guitar lesson at her friend's house. Her friend showed her a couple of notes, and before long, Lorena was playing the guitar by ear, pouring her soul into the melodies she created. She did the same the first time her fingers hit the piano keys.

She excelled academically too and became very involved in a variety of extracurricular activities at school. Though she didn't take to athletics as I had, Lorena did enjoy a run at both volleyball and cheerleading. She was also very good at drawing and earned several ribbons at the county fair for her creations. Performing in her first high school talent show brought her musical skills into the public realm for the first time, and she really began to shine.

Lorena's senior year seemed to be one long string of successes, and it was a joy for us to witness. Toward the end of that year, she was invited to sing in a trio at a Methodist church a few miles from Trenton.

"Mom, are you going to come hear me?" she asked a few days before the performance.

"Of course, Lo-lo," I said, "we'll be there."

It was hard for me to believe Lorena's childhood was coming to an end. She was no longer the little girl whose natural cuteness and sweet personality caused people to stop in admiration as I pushed her in the stroller through town.

But of all her gifts, her spiritual integrity is the one for which I am most grateful. This quality was exhibited recently when she quietly commented on the lack of opportunity for meditation during Mass. "They don't give me enough time to pray, Mom", she said.

Indeed, God has been very good to us in the gift of Lorena.

On the day her trio sang at the Methodist church, Philip wriggled in my lap as I watched the young musicians share their exuberant music.

I couldn't help but be in awe. In some ways, it was becoming harder for me to relate to where Lorena was in her life now. By the time I had turned eighteen, her current age, I was already a mother struggling through a life demanding instant maturity. Old dreams had died, but new dreams for Lorena had begun to take their place. Now they were unfolding before my eyes.

At the end of the service, a woman who had been sitting just a few rows ahead of us approached me and said, "Ramona?"

I recognized her right away. She had been a year behind me in school. But like the rest of my school pals, she had either drifted away after my exit or been pushed away by my ex.

"Hey, long time no see", I said. "How have you been?"

"Oh, great", she said. "I just have to say, I was looking at one of the girls singing, thinking how talented and gorgeous she is, and then I saw you; and it dawned on me that she must be your daughter."

"Yep, that's Lorena", I said. "She was invited here to sing today with her friends." We stood there for a while catching up. I shared with her what I had been doing in the pro-life ministry, and she listened with interest.

"You know, Ramona, I have to admit something to you. Back when I found out you were pregnant, I remember thinking, 'Ramona is so pretty and talented, and now she's ruined her life. That's too bad.' But now, seeing your daughter, I can't help but realize how wrong I was. You didn't ruin your life at all."

"Thanks," I said, "that means a lot to me. We are pretty proud of her."

It was a special moment for me, learning that someone from my old world was seeing what I had known for a while now.

Truth be told, I can't imagine my life without Lorena. No career, diploma, or degree can take the place of bringing a brand-new soul into the world and then seeing that soul flourish. It was the greatest feeling imaginable, and I was finally allowing myself to experience that blessing fully.

A month later, while helping Lorena pin on her graduation cap, I felt a swirl of emotions as I stood back and admired her in the shiny attire. "Looking good, Lo-lo girl", I said.

"Thanks, Mama," she said, "and by the way, I just want you to know that when I get my rose tonight, I'm giving it to Eugene."

At the graduation ceremony later, Lorena and the rest of her class would each be receiving a rose to be given to a parent. Without any prompting or guidance, Lorena had chosen to honor Eugene with her rose, even though Lucio would be in the crowd.

Despite the pain of growing up without her father, Lorena has always been fair-minded and respectful toward Lucio as the other person who brought her into the world. But she was also insistent upon giving credit where due, and this time she was indicating that Eugene was most worthy of the rose for his provision, presence, and constancy in her life.

As I watched Lorena accept an honors medal and four academic scholarships in the gym later that day, tears began charging to the surface. It was as if all of the pain and the joy I had experienced throughout her life, including the difficult years as a single mother, were converging. "No other parent here could possibly be feeling what I'm feeling right now", I thought.

Every statistic indicated that Lorena would end up a teen mother. Instead she turned into a young woman of virtue who has made some difficult choices of her own, including breaking a boy's heart—and her own in the process—for the sake of her future. She was everything I couldn't have hoped to have been at her age.

As she handed the rose to Eugene, I was vividly aware that this moment had come only by the grace of God. In a way, that moment was my medal, my diploma, for what I had done to raise her as well as possible, despite my mistakes.

I've protected you so long, sweetie, and you are precious to me, but now, you're entering the adult world, and it's time for you to fly.

Sitting next to Eugene, I looked at the rose in his hand and all that it represented. Wiping my tears, I squeezed his arm and whispered, "I love you."

* * * * *

Each of my children represents a unique time in my life and faith journey. Just as Philip, or "Little Turkey" as we call him, always brings smiles and joy, reminding me daily of how he helped me to discover my true purpose and a greater trust in God, Elijah has his own special place in my heart too.

Elijah literally means "The Lord is my God." He's my spunky survivor boy, my guy with all the questions and deep thoughts. He's not always the easiest to parent, but I can't help but love him to pieces. After all, he reminds me the most of myself.

Recently, Elijah walked into my bedroom and asked if I was still awake. Hearing me respond, he nestled close to me and said, "Mommy, do you want grandchildren someday?"

"Well, of course," I said, "I would love grandchildren."

"Okay, don't worry, Mommy. I won't let my wife kill my babies."

Shocked, I replied, "Well, son, hopefully you won't ever marry a woman who would want to kill your babies. I hope that you'll marry someone who shares your beliefs."

"But what if she goes behind my back?" he asked.

I had never discussed the pro-life versus pro-choice world with Elijah openly, nor had I tried to indoctrinate him in any way. His words had come from a pure heart and the messages of our culture. This is what our young men are being exposed to, I thought.

Elijah will have big battles to fight too, I realized at that moment. Even at the young age of six, he is justice-minded and understands that a woman's "right to choose" could leave him voiceless and helpless. He'll definitely need to lean hard on God to meet the increasingly divisive challenges of our culture. But I'll be around to guide him, along with Eugene and other faithful people in his life. He won't be alone.

The only response I could offer him that night, however, was, "That wouldn't happen, honey. Mommy wouldn't let that happen." For now, that would have to suffice.

As much as I adore both my sweet boys, however, it was their sister, Lorena, who first taught me the meaning of the words *sacrifice* and *love*.

Each time I hear her sing like a songbird, each note she strums on her guitar, each poem that erupts from her soul is part of a song that, to me, is Lorena's Song—the song of life.

18

Redeemed

Redemption can be defined as the act of saving or being saved from sin, error, or evil; the word can refer to God's plan for the redemption of his world. In the following story, as in the story of my life, both definitions are revealed.

In Luke 7:36–8:3, Jesus accepts an invitation by a Pharisee, Simon, to dine in his home. Upon learning that Jesus is dining there, a woman from the city, who is described as "sinful", also goes to the Pharisee's house with an alabaster flask of ointment.

Upon meeting Jesus at this place, the woman stands behind him at his feet and begins weeping. She then bathes his feet with her tears and wipes them with her hair. Then, in an act of utter humility, she kisses Jesus' feet and anoints them.

The Pharisee who had invited Jesus mutters to himself, "If this man were a prophet, he would have known who and what sort of woman this is who is touching him, for she is a sinner."

Jesus responds with a story of two people in debt to a creditor: one who owed five hundred days' wages and the other, fifty. "When they could not pay," Jesus says, "he forgave them both. Now which of them will love him more?"

"The one, I suppose, to whom he forgave more", Simon replies.

"You have judged rightly", Jesus says.

Then, turning to the woman, Jesus says to Simon, "Do you see this woman? I entered your house, you gave me no water for my feet, but she has wet my feet with her tears and wiped them with her hair. You gave me no kiss, but from the time I came in she has not ceased to kiss my feet. You did not anoint my head with oil, but she has anointed my feet with ointment. Therefore I tell you, her sins, which are many, are forgiven, for she loved much; but he who is forgiven little, loves little."

At that, Jesus turns to the woman and says, "Your sins are forgiven."

The others in attendance mumble to one another, "Who is this, who even forgives sins?"

Jesus then says to the woman, "Your faith has saved you; go in peace."

Your faith has saved you.

What sweet, beautiful words. They are the words of redemption. And they are words that resound in my heart now and every day as I think back on my journey.

I am the woman wiping Jesus' feet, humbled by my inadequacies yet filled with his forgiveness and grace. We all are that woman, wanting only to get a little closer to God.

At some point each of us finds himself wandering away from God. Our life's mission is to find our way back to him. But I've learned that God cannot extend mercy until we are willing to admit our wrongs and say, "Lord, I know that I've offended you." And we must experience true remorse. God already knows what we've done, after all. But he can't do anything about it until we've approached him, verbalized it, and asked for forgiveness.

When our kids lie to us, we might suspect they're lying, or even have proof, yet it's important that they fess up on their own. Until we hear them name their offense, we can't offer them true reconciliation. When they own up, then we can hug them and say, "Thank you for being truthful. I love you so much."

No wonder confession has become so important to me. I had resisted meeting Jesus in the confessional on many occasions out of fear. But God already knew what I had done wrong. I needed to discover that bringing my sins to the fore would make them more real, not to him but to me, and I needed to learn that the mercy he offered in turn would also become more real.

Though the woman in Scripture could have let fear prevent her from seeking Jesus, in the end, she was drawn to his love and felt the need for forgiveness. All other considerations fell away as she ran to him and, uninvited, entered a stranger's home. Despite her vulnerable state, she released her tears publicly, showing true remorse and a desire to be united with her Lord.

I too was propelled by an attraction to love, and once I reconnected with this beautiful, eternal source—first through Catholic radio and eventually through believers bearing quiet witness—I wanted more.

Even if it meant I would have to enter the homes of strangers, I wanted to see and to know more, no matter what it took or how my life might change. I was convinced that any change would be worth attaining the peace that had eluded me for so long.

And sure enough, once I began moving away from my sin, light began pouring in. "And God said, 'Let there be light'; and there was light. And God saw that the light was good; and God separated the light from the darkness" (Gen 1:3–4).

Without light, we cannot see earthly or spiritual matter.

In his first encyclical, *The Light of Faith*, Pope Francis said it is urgent that we see that faith is a light, for once the flame of faith dies out, so do all the other lights. "The light of faith is unique," he said, "since it is capable of illuminating every aspect of human existence."

The pope wrote that a light this powerful cannot come from us but must emanate from a primordial source: "In a word, it must come from God", he said, noting that faith is born from an encounter with the living God, who calls us and reveals his love.

"Transformed by this love, we gain fresh vision, new eyes to see; we realize that it contains a great promise of fulfillment, and a vision of the future opens up before us", the pope said. "Faith, received from God as a supernatural gift, becomes a light for our way, guiding our journey through time."

At a recent Mass, our priest reminded us how easily we can get off course in the dark. We might pray fervently without apparent result, he said, and wonder why God isn't answering us and choose to believe he doesn't exist. Or we might respond by placing our trust in God all the more and, in surrendering all to him, learn to rely not on our own efforts but on God.

"Life will never go our way until we learn this kind of surrender", our priest concluded.

During my days at Planned Parenthood, I would see a problem that needed fixing and charge in to fix it. "I'll make things happen", I would say, believing I could solve any issue that presented itself. But in the end, I didn't prove anything except that I had worked myself into a frazzle. And almost always, I would end up feeling used.

It took me a while to separate dark from light. Our society makes it very hard. The partying, fancy clothes, and shiny cars that woo us may fulfill our short-term desires but can never fulfill our true needs.

Yet many of us are willing to go to extremes to find fulfillment. We might even choose to do something gravely wrong to get ahead in life. "It's not such a big deal", we tell ourselves. "It's just one night" or "It's only a blob of tissue."

Whether we are taking part in an abortion or in another sin, we have convinced ourselves that achieving our dreams is worth whatever terrible act we think we must do. But we are left with a gnawing emptiness inside. Our goals, after all, have been achieved at the expense of something or someone else.

At this point, we can easily lose our belief in the good of the world and its people. We might become prone to cynicism and a persistent broken heart.

When I finally let go of all that I couldn't control and let God take the reins, real, lasting joy finally came into view. And for the first time in my life, I began to feel a deep and abiding satisfaction. We still struggle financially and worry about our family and how the future will play out. There are good and bad days, just as always, but there is peace.

Your faith has saved you; go in peace.

Amen, Lord. Thank you!

Now, standing more assuredly in the light, I understand how some of my suffering was the result of my own actions. But I've also come to see that Christ wants to help us through these difficult times and to bless us—all of us. He just asks that we follow him and his word.

* * * * *

As I look in the mirror, I squint, looking again for the girl I used to know, the one who climbed atop a roof one storm-threatened night.

At first, I see only the Ramona who has been through a bad situation and become jaded. "It's not too late", I remind her.

And then I see the younger version of her rushing past, running toward something—some*one*. I smile. I know where she's heading—back into God's arms.

It has taken time and a lot of tenderness, but I've finally discovered that the little girl inside me is worthy not only of life but of love. And it is she who has put in me a sense of urgency to share my story with others so that they too will search for light.

Just as she found, it's never too late to start over and to do the right thing, but thinking about it isn't enough. We must follow up with action even when it's difficult. And we must be prepared to fall a few times. When we place our trust in God, he will pick us up and send us back on our way with renewed confidence.

It's worth the trouble. As I've learned, every light-filled step brings us one step closer to the only true sanctuary: God's arms. And when at last we find ourselves there, enveloped in love, we'll realize with one long sigh of relief that our faith has indeed saved us and we have been redeemed.

EPILOGUE

In April 2013 we were coming to the end of Lorena's high school career, starting baseball season for Elijah, and keeping up with his increasingly mobile and curious little brother, Philip. Throw in the writing of a book, and it's no wonder I didn't have much time to keep up with current events. But toward the end of that month, a publicized trial drew my attention to a news story I couldn't ignore.

Many in our country became acquainted during this time with the name Kermit Gosnell, a late-term abortionist from Philadelphia charged with the murder of a woman and several infants.

Learning the sordid details of what had gone on at his facility, dubbed by some the "House of Horrors", my heart broke over the victims, including a mother and three precious babies who had died at his hands. The babies were distinguished not by name but by a letter, and I wondered, "How could this have happened?"

I also couldn't push away the haunting question that kept coming at me. *If this is the end, what is the beginning?* It didn't take long for me to find the answer. It was right within my own experiences.

This is the end of the beginning I helped to facilitate at Planned Parenthood. It was true. The mindset I had bought into while working there was the seed—a seed that has the potential to reach this kind of gruesome end. For when the contraception mentality pervades, so does the devaluation of human life, followed by abortion, and inevitably, infanticide.

During this time, many from both the pro-life and the pro-choice camps proclaimed the inhumanity of Gosnell's actions, but the more I watched, the more I wondered if this man wasn't simply a national scapegoat for a society that had lost its way long ago.

Seeing Gosnell's deadly work play out on television, I felt even more motivation and urgency to push forward with my story. If Gosnell's operation is the end point, I decided, I needed to address the beginning, to flash a warning signal to others.

Forty years before Gosnell, our nation chose, through the Supreme Court decision *Roe v. Wade*, a legal way to justify the killing of our youngest citizens. Like Gosnell, that case didn't appear out of thin air. It emerged because society had already begun orienting itself toward what Pope John Paul II termed the culture of death.

I recently learned that this great spiritual leader, who influenced my own journey in so many ways and who recently was canonized a saint, helped to formulate the prophetic and controversial encyclical letter *Humanae Vitae* (*Of Human Life*), published by his predecessor Pope Paul VI in 1968—five years before *Roe v. Wade*.

Through this letter, Pope Paul VI predicted that a wider acceptance of contraception would result in a lower regard for human life, leading to rampant sexual promiscuity and abuse, the breakdown of the family, and abortion.

The current number of deaths by abortion, the staggering incidences of sexually transmitted diseases, the number of broken families and troubled marriages are all the undeniable and tragic proof that contraception has been anything but the liberation it promises. In embracing the idea that separating the pleasurable and procreative aspects of sexual intimacy will make us freer, we have become more enslaved than ever.

Many of the faith-filled have been among those who have bought into this deception, though often innocently. I was among them, and now that I see, I cannot ignore my responsibility to suggest that what was foretold four decades ago deserves a second look.

If we're to reverse these disturbing trends, we must be honest with ourselves. And honesty begins with the facts, including the fifty-five million dead babies in the forty years since *Roe v. Wade*. We must face that contraception hasn't come close to living up to its original claim of keeping abortions rare and safe.

Lately we have been told that efforts to limit abortion or to allow religious employers not to fund abortion-causing drugs represent a "War on Women". Yes, there is a war, but it's a war on womanhood, motherhood, and marriage, waged by the makers and the providers of contraception.

The majority of Catholics agree that abortion is morally wrong, but many go against Church teaching regarding the use of contraception. I believe this is largely because people don't understand why the Church teaches against it, and they've missed its connection with abortion. Even if it's inconvenient and makes us feel uneasy, we need to consider the facts about contraception and abortion and then compare them against the Church's wisdom.

For example, by disrupting a woman's hormonal balance, oral or implanted contraceptives can be detrimental to a woman's health. And these are designed not only to prevent conception but, if conception occurs, to prevent a new human life from implanting in the womb.

On the other hand, when used correctly, Natural Family Planning is as effective as these contraceptives in preventing conception, yet without harming the woman's health or destroying a new human life. Unlike contraception, Natural Family Planning allows both husband and wife to give of themselves completely, with their fertility intact, in the marital embrace. It requires both of them to accept the responsibility for bringing children into the world. With facts like these in mind, the Church's vision for marriage as a lifelong, faithful, and fruitful union of a husband and a wife is positively inspiring.

If not for my work with Planned Parenthood, I may never have confronted the issue of artificial birth control or even thought twice about it. After all, I was a contraceptive user as well, making sure to take my pill every night before I went to bed. But through my experiences there, God graced me with the wisdom to spot the dangers of widespread contraceptive use and allowed me, through firsthand observations, to see the tie between contraception and abortion.

When referring to artificial birth control in *Humanae Vitae*, Pope Paul VI wrote that people, especially young people who are particularly vulnerable to temptation, "need incentives to keep the moral law, and it is an evil thing to make it easy for them to break that law."

Unfortunately, Planned Parenthood and other providers of contraception and abortion have done exactly this—made it exceedingly easy for young people to break the moral law. The wider culture aids and abets them in this. Sex in whatever circumstances they choose is being sold to them through television, movies, radio, billboards, the Internet, cell phone apps, video games, and even restaurants. Young people are pressured to have premarital sex by their friends, boyfriends, and girlfriends, and by sex education programs in schools.

Sex sells, and Planned Parenthood knows it. It promotes sexual promiscuity as a means for achieving happiness instead of promoting sexual self-control. It tells the unmarried, and even teenagers, that by using contraception they are being smart about sex because they are preventing unwanted pregnancies.

The facts tell a different story. The Guttmacher Institute, the research arm for Planned Parenthood, revealed that one in ten women will have an abortion by age twenty. Of those seeking abortion in the United States, 18 percent are teenagers, and women in their twenties account for more than half of all abortions. And according to the same research, 54 percent of women who have had abortions used a contraceptive method, usually a condom or a pill, during the month they became pregnant.

From a non-spiritual perspective alone, these statistics scream at us that unmarried young people should not be engaging in sexual activity. Yet somehow we've bought into the idea that it's good to prepare our young people early for their sexual lives by passing out free condoms and telling them that since they're going to do it anyway they might as well be "safe".

The following passage of *Humanae Vitae,* perhaps its most prophetic, brings to light the consequences of contraception in marriage:

> Let them first consider how easily this course of action could open wide the way for marital infidelity and a general lowering of moral standards. Another effect that gives cause for alarm is that a man who grows accustomed to the use of contraceptive methods may forget the reverence due to a woman, and, disregarding her physical and emotional equilibrium, reduce her to being a mere instrument for the satisfaction of his own desires, no longer considering her as his partner whom he should surround with care and affection.

Contraceptives open the door for sexual immorality, plain and simple. Since the legalization of contraception and abortion, sexual immorality has skyrocketed, and I witnessed it in a jarring way during my work for Planned Parenthood, by observing teenagers "hooking up" at the rate of three new partners a month and watching young girls returning with recurring STDs. This seems like sex education gone wrong to me.

So where does abortion come in? *Humanae Vitae* mentions that the contraceptive mentality encourages a man to "forget the reverence due to a woman", reducing her to an object to satisfy his own desires. When a woman uses contraception, she is subliminally agreeing to this. By entering into a union that is based on a false premise, she is setting herself up for being wounded. By agreeing to the pleasure of sex without consequences, she is expressing an attitude that is closed to life and opening herself to being used rather than truly loved, respected, and honored for her life-giving potential.

Even with contraception, an unwanted pregnancy sometimes happens. At that point, a woman is often forced down a difficult and lonely path. If she is young and unmarried, she often must choose between raising the baby alone because the man she had sex with is not ready to be a father, giving the baby up for adoption, or having an abortion. Abortion has now become an option.

What about married people having an affair? What happens when the condom breaks or slips off, or when a mistress lies about taking her birth control pill? How does the man tell his wife that his mistress is pregnant? How does a wife tell her husband that she is carrying someone else's child? Abortion has now become an option.

Contraceptives fail, and when they do, women and men often resort to abortion. Taking into consideration that half of all pregnancies are unintended, and four in ten are terminated, it's no wonder that we've reached the fifty-five-million-abortion mark in forty years.

We were not created to be mere objects of pleasure. God did not create us to be used by one another as such. God created sex to be both procreative and pleasurable within the context of marriage for the same reason he gives us any commandment—not to restrict us but to protect us from harm.

When we experience sex outside of marriage, there are emotional, psychological, and physical consequences. They can come in the form of heartbreak, low self-esteem, shame, guilt, STDs, and unplanned pregnancy. God knows this and established sex within marriage for that very reason.

When we seek pleasure rather than joy, as we often are tempted to do, we set ourselves up for a life of pain and the destruction of our souls. Sex is designed to be pleasurable, but when it takes place outside of marriage, it loses its meaning, purpose, and beauty. There is no "I love you forever and always." There is no commitment. We are objects of pleasure, and when that reality sets in, we move on to the next fix to fill the empty void.

Joy, however, does last, and Christ is the ultimate giver of this gift. When we have the love of Christ, nothing in the world can rob us of our joy and peace.

The message I ultimately wish to bring is not one of despair, for even when we make mistakes, as I have, God never abandons us. When we search for him, we find him. When we cry out to him, he hears us. When we lose our way, he waits patiently for us to find our way back to him, with loving arms extended and an endless ocean of mercy at the ready.

I've lost my way more than once, always when I lost sight of my worth in God's eyes. I gave up my virginity, became pregnant, and yet held on to the hope that I could find a way back into God's good grace. I then spent years using contraception, believing I was doing nothing wrong and was still a good Catholic. I was lost mainly because of my lack of knowledge and understanding.

Then, while working for Planned Parenthood, I drifted further and further away from my faith. I bought into the contraceptive mentality and found myself submerged deeper and deeper in deception. It was then that I became more accepting of abortion and a woman's "right to choose". Eventually, I had to struggle again to find my way to the surface in the ocean of sin in which I was drowning. But like countless times before, God was there, waiting for me at the shore.

God is waiting for us all to follow him and to choose him so that he can bless us and give us the peace we long for in our lives. His love, mercy, and forgiveness are endless. It was his mercy that redeemed me, allowing me to start again.

Like rainwater falling on a parched desert land, God's mercy washes away our sins and brings life back to our dry and barren souls.

ADDENDUM

Looking back at my life as a child, I can see that even though it was not ideal, it's very obvious that I was loved.

When I became pregnant at sixteen, I learned the meaning of unconditional love. It was unconditional love that made it possible for me to say yes to my pregnancy. It was that same love that ruled out the possibility of abortion. *Abortion* was not a word we had ever used in our house, nor considered.

Reflecting back, it makes sense why I would be so willing to sacrifice my life for the life of my baby. Although my parents had their struggles, they taught my sister and me the meaning of love and sacrifice through their actions. My mother always put our needs before her own, making sure our basic needs of food and clothing were always met. She did the very best she could with her situation. My father, though suffering from his own demons, always came through for our family when we needed him the most and found a way to provide. He never turned his back on me when I made bad choices or made life difficult.

Both parents taught me the meaning of love and faith in an unconventional kind of way, by welcoming a grandchild without batting an eye. God had always provided for us so why would this time be any different? Their daughter was having a baby, and there was nothing else to be said about it. If only other young women could have parents as forgiving as mine.

Though I didn't always see this as I was growing up, now I see two people who struggled to stay faithful to the sacrament of marriage and tried hard to love their two girls. There are no perfect parents, and I take the best of what I learned from my mom and dad, do what I can to implement it, and work on leaving the negatives in the past. I'm not always successful, but my parents' example of love, sacrifice, and faith keeps me holding on with all my might.

Despite the imperfection, despite the pain of my growing-up years, I did grow up, and by the grace of God, I learned the meaning of forgiveness and love. I wouldn't be who or where I am today if it weren't for my mom and dad.

ACKNOWLEDGMENTS

No book comes into the world single-handedly. Rather, a community gathers round to help what often begins as the interior yearning of a soul to become a life-giving witness to the world. We count ourselves abundantly blessed by all who have encircled us protectively throughout this project, especially by covering us in their prayers.

The book began with a nudge from Molly Fitzgerald, then development director for Guadalupe Radio Network, who heard Ramona's story and urged a wider sharing. As Ramona discerned this possibility, she and Lauren Muzyka began searching for a writer, which led them to Teresa Tomeo, Catholic radio host, and eventually to Lisa Hendey of CatholicMom.com. Lisa suggested one of her contributing writers, Roxane, and from this divine web, the story sprang to life.

As our first draft reached completion, the Nelson family kindly opened their home in Frisco, Texas, so that we could gather with a group of supporters and share our opening chapter. There, we received both spiritual and financial reinforcement, along with a generous lead that brought us to Ignatius Press.

Lauren Muzyka—her prayers, great memory, good heart, and unfettered optimism—brought so much to this project from the beginning. She was the glue that held us together, the third prong in our little trinitarian effort that has come to fruition at last. We cannot thank her enough. Peter Muzyka lived up to his name, providing a sturdy, steady source of support that buoyed us all.

In both Texas and North Dakota and beyond, pockets of prayer warriors silently but powerfully lifted us up in ways we will not fully know this side of heaven. Though we cannot name them all in this small space, we are grateful to all as this story continues to make an impact.

One from Wisconsin, however, must not go without mention. After Ramona's speaking engagement in Green Lake, this woman of prayer shared that the Holy Spirit had directed her to give Ramona all the money in her purse. Coming at a particularly tight time financially, the money enabled Ramona to make the trip home. This benefactor was one among many unnamed but not forgotten angels on earth, along with those who helped Ramona to transition out of Planned Parenthood.

Others who stepped forward in an especially tangible way include Gerry and Colleen Brundage, who first welcomed Ramona and later made a special place in their hearts for her; Joseph, Mary, and Paul Borchard, whose constant prayers offered needed strength for the journey; Karen and Jeremy Nelson, who supported this project in myriad ways; and Becky Viosky, whose astuteness and assurance was life-saving. Ellen Rossini offered skilled, gracious guidance that helped this story to emerge, and Aurora Tinajero shared her needed wisdom. We also have been touched by the quiet sacrifices of Angela Heiter and John Bezner, whose very special gifts to Ramona and her family will be long remembered. Thank you also to Dave Palmer of Guadalupe Radio in Dallas–Fort Worth and Steve Splonskowski of Real Presence Radio in Fargo–Moorhead and their respective staffs, who offered air time and encouragement; and to David Bereit and Shawn Carney, for their saving ministry and direction.

We also want to thank, in Texas, Karen Garnett, Patty Sherrod, Chris and Jessica Leminger, Chris and Bonnie Pendergrass, Omar Aguilar, Elizabeth Reyes, Diane Xavier, Gracie Sanford, Kevin and Jorja Baumgarten, Carl and Katharine Oehmann, Rob and Maddie Muzyka, Elizabeth and Danny Muzyka and Brian and Maria Kahlig—their support gave us what we needed to push through to the end.

On the North Dakota end, Mother Joseph Marie and the good sisters at the Carmel of Mary Monastery in Wahpeton provided Roxane an indispensable refuge. Additionally, all of these friends contributed vital reinforcement: Mary Dosch, Sharon Gunwall, Father Kurtis Gunwall, Linda Morris, Beverly Salonen, Colleen Samson, Mary Kay Schott, and Vicky Westra, along with the Shanley Teens for Life parents, Marriage Encounter, and Tuesday faith-sharing groups.

As busy mothers, we would have been stymied without the sacrificial efforts of our husbands, Eugene and Troy, who held down the forts during our absences from home and gave unfaltering emotional support. Our nine children have been our most fervent cheerleaders and helped to inspire our shared desire to highlight the riches of the Catholic faith.

Ramona could not have come so far without her parents and her extended family nearby, including her sister, Priscella, who was always there as a silent supporter and through all her stages of motherhood. Roxane's mother, Jane, and her sister Camille, also have watched prayerfully from the wings, fortifying us with their encouraging words. And while he left this world in the middle of our work, Roxane's father, Robert Beauclair, lover of words and teller of stories, whispered his influence into this project often.

Though we have left them to the end, their part in this is unequaled. And so, on bended knees, we wish to thank our Blessed Mother, Saints Teresa Benedicta of the Cross, Bernadette, and Faustina, along with the whole cloud of witnesses who gathered around us, gently wiping the sweat from our brows and consoling us in our worry over our families. And finally, with a tandem bow, we give thanks and praise to God. This story has been his from the beginning, and we offer it back to him now, with the hopes that through it, he will move others' hearts as much as he has ours.

With our deepest appreciation, Ramona and Roxane.